On
the Political

Praise for the series

'. . . allows a space for distinguished thinkers to write about their passions.'
The Philosophers' Magazine

'. . . deserve high praise.'
Boyd Tonkin, *The Independent* (UK)

'This is clearly an important series. I look forward to receiving future volumes.'
Frank Kermode, author of *Shakespeare's Language*

'both rigorous and accessible.'
Humanist News

'the series looks superb.'
Quentin Skinner

'. . . an excellent and beautiful series.'
Ben Rogers, author of *A.J. Ayer: A Life*

'Routledge's *Thinking in Action* series is the theory junkie's answer to the eminently pocketable Penguin 60s series.'
Mute Magazine (UK)

'Routledge's new series, *Thinking in Action*, brings philosophers to our aid . . .'
The Evening Standard (UK)

'. . . a welcome series by Routledge.'
Bulletin of Science, Technology and Society (Can)

CHANTAL MOUFFE

On the Political

LONDON AND NEW YORK

First published 2005
by Routledge
2 Park Square, Milton Park, Abingdon, OX14 4RN

Simultaneously published in the USA and Canada
by Routledge
270 Madison Ave, New York, NY 10016

Reprinted 2006 (twice), 2007, 2008

Routledge is an imprint of the Taylor & Francis Group, an informa business

© 2005 Chantal Mouffe

Typeset in Joanna MT by
RefineCatch Ltd, Bungay, Suffolk
Printed and bound in Great Britain by
TJ International, Padstow, Cornwall

British Library Cataloguing in Publication Data
A catalogue record for this book is available from the British Library

Library of Congress Cataloging in Publication Data
Mouffe, Chantal.
    On the political / Chantal Mouffe.
        p. cm—(Thinking in action)
    Includes bibliographical references.
    1. Political science—Philosophy.   2. Democracy.   3. Right and left (Political
science)   I. Title.   II. Series.
JA71.M679 2005
320.5—dc22   2004024746

ISBN10: 0-415-30520-9 (hbk)
ISBN10: 0-415-30521-7 (pbk)

ISBN13: 978-0-415-30520-4 (hbk)
ISBN13: 978-0-415-30521-1 (pbk)

One

In this book I want to take issue with the view which informs the 'common sense' in a majority of Western societies: the idea that the stage of economico-political development that we have now reached constitutes a great progress in the evolution of humanity and that we should celebrate the possibilities that it opens. Sociologists claim that we have entered a 'second modernity' in which individuals liberated from collective ties can now dedicate themselves to cultivating a diversity of lifestyles, unhindered by antiquated attachments. The 'free world' has triumphed over communism and, with the weakening of collective identities, a world 'without enemies' is now possible. Partisan conflicts are a thing of the past and consensus can now be obtained through dialogue. Thanks to globalization and the universalization of liberal democracy, we can expect a cosmopolitan future bringing peace, prosperity and the implementation of human rights worldwide.

I want to challenge this 'post-political' vision. My main target will be those in the progressive camp who accept this optimistic view of globalization and have become the advocates of a consensual form of democracy. Scrutinizing some of the fashionable theories which underpin the post-political Zeitgeist in a series of fields – sociology, political theory and international relations – I will argue that such an approach is profoundly mistaken and that, instead of contributing to a 'democratization of democracy', it is at the origin of many of the problems that democratic institutions are currently facing. Notions such as 'partisan-free democracy', 'dialogic democracy', 'cosmopolitan democracy', 'good governance', 'global civil society', 'cosmopolitan sovereignty', 'absolute democracy' – to quote only a few of the currently fashionable notions – all partake of a common anti-political vision which refuses to acknowledge the antagonistic dimension constitutive of 'the political'. Their aim is the establishment of a world 'beyond left and right', 'beyond hegemony', 'beyond sovereignty' and 'beyond antagonism'. Such a longing reveals a complete lack of understanding of what is at stake in democratic politics and of the dynamics of constitution of political identities and, as we will see, it contributes to exacerbating the antagonistic potential existing in society.

A significant part of my argument will consist in examining the consequences of the negation of antagonism in several areas, both in theory and in politics. It is my contention that envisaging the aim of democratic politics in terms of consensus and reconciliation is not only conceptually mistaken, it is also fraught with political dangers. The aspiration to a world where the we/they discrimination would have been overcome is based on flawed premises and those who share such a vision are bound to miss the real task facing democratic politics.

To be sure this blindness to antagonism is not new. Democratic theory has long been informed by the belief that the inner goodness and original innocence of human beings was a necessary condition for asserting the viability of democracy. An idealized view of human sociability, as being essentially moved by empathy and reciprocity, has generally provided the basis of modern democratic political thinking. Violence and hostility are seen as an archaic phenomenon, to be eliminated thanks to the progress of exchange and the establishment, through a social contract, of a transparent communication among rational participants. Those who challenged this optimistic view were automatically perceived as enemies of democracy. Few attempts have been made to elaborate the democratic project on an anthropology which acknowledges the ambivalent character of human sociability and the fact that reciprocity and hostility cannot be dissociated. And despite what we have learned through different disciplines, the optimistic anthropology is still prevalent today. For instance, more than half a century after Freud's death, the resistance to psychoanalysis in political theory is still very strong and its lessons about the ineradicability of antagonism have not yet been assimilated.

I contend that the belief in the possibility of a universal rational consensus has put democratic thinking on the wrong track. Instead of trying to design the institutions which, through supposedly 'impartial' procedures, would reconcile all conflicting interests and values, the task for democratic theorists and politicians should be to envisage the creation of a vibrant 'agonistic' public sphere of contestation where different hegemonic political projects can be confronted. This is, in my view, the *sine qua non* for an effective exercise of democracy. There is much talk today of 'dialogue' and 'deliberation' but what is the meaning of such words in the political field, if no real choice is at hand and if the participants in the discussion are not able to decide between clearly differentiated alternatives?

I have no doubt that the liberals who think that rational

agreement can be reached in politics, and who see democratic institutions as the vehicle for finding the rational answer to the different problems of society, will accuse my conception of the political of being 'nihilistic'. And so will those on the ultra-left who believe in the possibility of an 'absolute democracy'. There is no point in trying to convince them that my agonistic approach is informed by the 'true' understanding of 'the political'. I will follow a different route. What I will do is bring to the fore the consequences for democratic politics of the denial of 'the political' as I define it. I will reveal how the consensual approach, instead of creating the conditions for a reconciled society, leads to the emergence of antagonisms that an agonistic perspective, by providing those conflicts with a legitimate form of expression, would have managed to avoid. In that way I hope to demonstrate that acknowledging the ineradicability of the conflictual dimension in social life, far from undermining the democratic project, is the necessary condition for grasping the challenge to which democratic politics is confronted.

Because of the rationalism prevalent in liberal political discourse, it is often among conservative theorists that I have found crucial insights for an adequate understanding of the political. They can better shake our dogmatic assumptions than liberal apologists. This is why I have chosen to conduct my critique of liberal thought under the aegis of such a controversial thinker as Carl Schmitt. I am convinced that there is much that we can learn from him, as one of the most brilliant and intransigent opponents of liberalism. I am perfectly aware that, because of Schmitt's compromise with nazism, such a choice might arouse hostility. Many people will find it rather perverse if not outright outrageous. Yet, I believe that it is the intellectual force of theorists, not their moral qualities, that should be the decisive criteria in deciding whether we need to establish a dialogue with their work.

I see the refusal of many democratic theorists to engage with Schmitt's thought on moral grounds as typical of the moralistic tendency which is characteristic of the post-political *Zeitgeist*. In fact, the critique of such tendency is at the core of my reflection. A central thesis of this book is that, contrary to what post-political theorists want us to believe, what we are currently witnessing is not the disappearance of the political in its adversarial dimension but something different. What is happening is that nowadays the political is played out in the *moral register*. In other words, it still consists in a we/they discrimination, but the we/they, instead of being defined with political categories, is now established in moral terms. In place of a struggle between 'right and left' we are faced with a struggle between 'right and wrong'.

In Chapter 4, using the examples of right-wing populism and of terrorism, I will examine the consequences of such a displacement for domestic as well as for international politics and unveil the dangers that it entails. My argument is that, when the channels are not available through which conflicts could take an 'agonistic' form, those conflicts tend to emerge on the antagonistic mode. Now, when instead of being formulated as a political confrontation between 'adversaries', the we/they confrontation is visualized as a moral one between good and evil, the opponent can be perceived only as an enemy to be destroyed and this is not conducive to an agonistic treatment. Hence the current emergence of antagonisms which put into question the very parameters of the existing order.

Another thesis concerns the nature of collective identities which always entail a we/they discrimination. They play a central part in politics and the task of democratic politics is not to overcome them through consensus but to construct them in a way that energizes the democratic confrontation. The mistake of liberal rationalism is to ignore the affective dimension mobilized by collective identifications and to imagine that those supposedly archaic 'passions' are bound to disappear with the advance of individualism and the progress of rationality. This is why democratic theory is so badly prepared to grasp the nature of 'mass' political movements as well as phenomena such as nationalism. The part played by 'passions' in politics reveals that, in order to come to terms with 'the political', it is not enough for liberal theory to acknowledge the existence of a plurality of values and to extol toleration. Democratic politics cannot be limited to establishing compromises among interests or values or to deliberation about the common good; it needs to have a real purchase on people's desires and fantasies. To be able to mobilize passions towards democratic designs, democratic politics must have a partisan character. This is indeed the function of the left/right distinction and we should resist the call by post-political theorists to think 'beyond left and right'.

There is a final lesson that we can draw from a reflection on 'the political'. If the possibility of reaching an order 'beyond hegemony' is foreclosed, what does that imply for the cosmopolitan project? Could it ever be more than the establishment of the world hegemony of a power which would have managed to conceal its rule by identifying its interests with those of humanity? Contrary to the numerous theorists who see the end of the bipolar system as bringing the hope of a cosmopolitan democracy, I will argue that the dangers entailed by the current unipolar order can be avoided only by the implementation of a multipolar world, with an equilibrium among several regional poles allowing for a plurality of hegemonic powers. This is the only way to avoid the hegemony of one single hyperpower.

In the realm of 'the political', Machiavelli's crucial insight is still worth meditating: 'In each city are found these two different desires ... the man of the people hates being ordered and oppressed by those greater than he. And the great like to order and oppress the people.' What defines the post-political perspective is the claim that we have entered a new era where this potential antagonism has disappeared. And this is why it can put in jeopardy the future of democratic politics.

Two

This chapter will delineate the theoretical framework which informs my critique of the current 'post-political' *Zeitgeist*. Its main tenets have been developed in several of my previous works[1] and here I will limit myself to the aspects which are relevant for the argument presented in this book. The most important concerns the distinction I propose to make between 'politics' and 'the political'. To be sure, in ordinary language, it is not very common to speak of 'the political' but I think that such a distinction opens important new paths for reflection and many political theorists are making it. The difficulty, though, is that no agreement exists among them concerning the meaning attributed to the respective terms and that may cause a certain confusion. Commonalities exist however which can provide some points of orientation. For instance to make this distinction suggests a difference between two types of approach: political science which deals with the empirical field of 'politics', and political theory which is the domain of philosophers who enquire not about facts of 'politics' but about the essence of 'the political'. If we wanted to express such a distinction in a philosophical way, we could, borrowing the vocabulary of Heidegger, say that politics refers to the 'ontic' level while 'the political' has to do with the 'ontological' one. This means that the ontic has to do with the manifold practices of conventional politics, while the ontological concerns the very way in which society is instituted.

But this still leaves the possibility of considerable disagreement about what constitutes 'the political'. Some theorists such as Hannah Arendt envisage the political as a space of freedom and public deliberation, while others see it as a space of power, conflict and antagonism. My understanding of 'the political' clearly belongs to the second perspective. More precisely this is how I distinguish between 'the political' and 'politics': by 'the political' I mean the dimension of antagonism which I take to be constitutive of human societies, while by 'politics' I mean the set of practices and institutions through which an order is created, organizing human coexistence in the context of conflictuality provided by the political.

My main field of enquiry in this book concerns the current practices of democratic politics and is therefore located at the 'ontic' level. But I contend that it is the lack of understanding of 'the political' in its ontological dimension which is at the origin of our current incapacity to think in a political way. Although an important part of my argument is of a theoretical nature, my central aim is a political one. I am convinced that what is at stake in the discussion about the nature of 'the political' is the very future of democracy. I intend to show how the rationalist approach dominant in democratic theory prevents us from posing the questions which are crucial for democratic politics. This is why we urgently need an alternative approach which will enable us to grasp the challenges with which democratic politics is today confronted.

THE POLITICAL AS ANTAGONISM

The point of departure of my enquiry is our current unability to envisage the problems facing our societies in a *political* way. What I mean by that is that political questions are not mere technical issues to be solved by experts. Properly political questions always involve decisions which require us to make a choice between conflicting alternatives. I will argue that this incapacity to think politically is to a great extent due to the uncontested hegemony of liberalism, and an important part of my reflection will be dedicated to examining the impact of liberal ideas in human sciences and in politics. My aim is to bring to the fore liberalism's central deficiency in the political field: its negation of the ineradicable character of antagonism. 'Liberalism', in the way I understand it in the present context, refers to a philosophical discourse with many variants, united not by a common essence but by a multiplicity of what Wittgenstein calls 'family resemblances'. There are to be sure many liberalisms, some more progressive than others, but with a few exceptions (Isaiah Berlin, Joseph Raz, John Gray, Michael Walzer among others) the dominant tendency in liberal thought is characterized by a rationalist and individualist approach which forecloses acknowledging the nature of collective identities. This kind of liberalism is unable to adequately grasp the pluralistic nature of the social world, with the conflicts that pluralism entails; conflicts for which no rational solution could ever exist. The typical liberal understanding of pluralism is that we live in a world in which there are indeed many perspectives and values and that, owing to empirical limitations, we will never be able to adopt them all, but that, when put together, they constitute an harmonious and non-conflictual ensemble. This is why this type of liberalism must negate the political in its antagonistic dimension.

The most radical challenge to liberalism, so understood, is found in the work of Carl Schmitt, whose provocative critique I will mobilize in my confrontation with liberal assumptions. In *The Concept of the Political*, Schmitt declares bluntly that the pure and rigorous principle of liberalism could not give birth to a specifically political conception. Every consistent individualism must, in his view, negate the political since it requires the individual to remain the ultimate point of reference. He states: 'In a very systematic fashion liberal thought evades or ignores state and politics and moves instead in a typical recurring polarity of two heterogeneous spheres, namely ethics and economics, intellect and trade, education and property. The critical distrust of state and politics is easily explained by the principles of a system whereby the individual must remain *terminus a quo* and *terminus ad quem*.'[2] The methodological individualism which characterizes liberal thought precludes understanding the nature of collective identities. Yet, for Schmitt, the criteria of the political, its *differentia specifica*, is the friend/enemy discrimination. It deals with the formation of a 'we' as opposed to a 'they' and is always concerned with collective forms of identification; it has to do with conflict and antagonism and is therefore the realm of decision, not free discussion. The political, as he puts it, 'can be understood only in the context of the friend/enemy grouping, regardless of the aspects which this possibility implies for morality, aesthetics and economics'.[3]

A key point of Schmitt's approach is that, by showing that every consensus is based on acts of exclusion, it reveals the impossibility of a fully inclusive 'rational' consensus. Now, as I indicated, next to individualism, the other central trait of most liberal thought is the rationalist belief in the availability of a universal consensus based on reason. It is therefore no wonder that the political constitutes its blind spot. The political cannot be grasped by liberal rationalism for the simple reason that every consistent rationalism requires negating the irreducibility of antagonism. Liberalism has to negate antagonism since, by bringing to the fore the inescapable moment of decision – in the strong sense of having to decide in an undecidable terrain – what antagonism reveals is the very limit of any rational consensus. As far as liberal thought adheres to individualism and rationalism, its blindness to the political in its antagonistic dimension is therefore not a mere empirical omission but a constitutive one.

Schmitt points out that 'there exists a liberal policy in the form of a polemical antithesis against state, church or other institutions which restrict individual freedom. There exists a liberal policy of trade, church and education, but absolutely no liberal politics, only a liberal critique of politics. The systematic theory of liberalism concerns almost solely the internal struggle against the power of the state.'[4] However, the liberal attempt to annihilate the political is, he says, bound to fail. The political can never be eradicated because it can derive its energy from the most varied human endeavours: 'every religious, moral, economic, ethical or other antithesis transforms itself into a political one if it is sufficiently strong to group human beings effectively according to friend and enemy'.[5]

The Concept of the Political was originally published in 1932, but Schmitt's critique is more relevant now than ever. If we examine the evolution of liberal thought since then, we ascertain that it has indeed moved between economics and ethics. Broadly speaking, we can today single out two main liberal paradigms. The first one, sometimes called 'aggregative', envisages politics as the establishment of a compromise between differing competing forces in society. Individuals are portrayed as rational beings, driven by the maximization of their own interests and as acting in the political world in a basically instrumental way. It is the idea of the market applied to the domain of politics which is apprehended with concepts borrowed from economics. The other paradigm, the 'deliberative', developed in reaction against this instrumentalist model, aims at creating a link between morality and politics. Its advocates want to replace instrumental rationality by communicative rationality. They present political debate as a specific field of application of morality and believe that it is possible to create in the realm of politics a rational moral consensus by means of free discussion. In this case politics is apprehended not through economics but through ethics or morality.

The challenge posed by Schmitt to the rationalist conception of the political is clearly acknowledged by Jürgen Habermas, one of the main advocates of the deliberative model, who tries to exorcize it by declaring that those who put into question the possibility of such a rational consensus and who affirm that politics is a domain where one should always expect to find discord undermine the very possibility of democracy. He asserts that 'If questions of justice cannot transcend the ethical self-understanding of competing forms of life, and if existentially relevant values, conflicts and oppositions must penetrate all controversial questions, then in the final analysis we will end up with something resembling Carl Schmitt's understanding of politics'.[6]

Contrary to Habermas and all those who affirm that such an understanding of the political is antithetical to the democratic project, I submit that Schmitt's emphasis on the ever present possibility of the friend/enemy distinction and the conflictual nature of politics constitutes the necessary starting point for envisaging the aims of democratic politics. Only by acknowledging 'the political' in its antagonistic dimension can we pose the central question for democratic politics. This question, *pace* liberal theorists, is not how to negotiate a compromise among competing interests, nor is it how to reach a 'rational', i.e. a fully inclusive, consensus, without any exclusion. Despite what many liberals want us to believe, the specificity of democratic politics is not the overcoming of the we/they opposition but the different way in which it is established. What democracy requires is drawing the we/they distinction in a way which is compatible with the recognition of the pluralism which is constitutive of modern democracy.

PLURALISM AND FRIEND/ENEMY RELATION

Of course, at this point we need to part company with Schmitt, who was adamant that there is no place for pluralism inside a democratic political community. Democracy, as he understood it, requires the existence of an homogeneous *demos*, and this precludes any possibility of pluralism. This is why he saw an insurmountable contradiction between liberal pluralism and democracy. For him, the only possible and legitimate pluralism is a pluralism of states. What I propose to do then is to think 'with Schmitt against Schmitt', using his critique of liberal individualism and rationalism to propose a new understanding of liberal democratic politics instead of following Schmitt in rejecting it.

In my view one of Schmitt's central insights is his thesis that political identities consist in a certain type of we/they relation, the relation friend/enemy which can emerge out of very diverse forms of social relations. By bringing to the fore the relational nature of political identities, he anticipates several currents of thought, such as post-structuralism, that will later stress the relational character of all identities. Today, thanks to those later theoretical developments, we are in a position to elaborate better what Schmitt forcefully asserted but left untheorized. The challenge for us is to develop his insights into a different direction and to visualize other understandings of the friend/enemy distinction, understandings compatible with democratic pluralism.

I have found the notion of the 'constitutive outside' particularly useful for such a project because it unveils what is at stake in the constitution of identity. This term has been proposed by Henry Staten[7] to refer to a number of themes developed by Jacques Derrida around notions such as 'supplement', 'trace' and 'différance'. The aim is to highlight the fact that the creation of an identity implies the establishment of a difference, difference which is often constructed on the basis of a hierarchy, for example between form and matter, black and white, man and woman, etc. Once we have understood that every identity is relational and that the affirmation of a difference is a precondition for the existence of any identity, i.e. the perception of something 'other' which constitutes its 'exterior', we are, I think, in a better position to understand Schmitt's point about the ever present possibility of antagonism and to see how a social relation can become the breeding ground for antagonism.

In the field of collective identities, we are always dealing with the creation of a 'we' which can exist only by the demarcation of a 'they'. This does not mean of course that such a relation is necessarily one of friend/enemy, i.e. an antagonistic one. But we should acknowledge that, in certain conditions, there is always the possibility that this we/they relation can *become* antagonistic, i.e. that it can turn into a relation of friend/enemy. This happens when the 'they' is perceived as putting into question the identity of the 'we' and as threatening its existence. From that moment on, as the case of the disintegration of Yugoslavia testifies, any form of we/they relation, whether religious, ethnic, economic or other, becomes the locus of an antagonism.

For Schmitt, of course, in order to be political this we/they relation had to take the antagonistic form of a friend/enemy relation. This is why he could not allow its presence within the political association. And he was no doubt right to warn against the dangers that an antagonistic pluralism entails for the permanence of the political entity. However, as I will argue in a moment, the friend/enemy distinction can be considered as merely one of the possible forms of expression of the antagonistic dimension which is constitutive of the political. We can also, while acknowledging the ever present possibility of antagonism, imagine other political modes of construction of the we/they. If we follow this route, we will realize that the challenge for democratic politics consists in trying to keep the emergence of antagonism at bay by establishing the we/they in a different way.

Before developing this point further, let us draw a first theoretical conclusion from the previous reflections. What we can assert at this stage is that the we/they distinction, which is the condition of possibility of formation of political identities, can always become the locus of an antagonism. Since all forms of political identities entail a we/they distinction, this means that the possibility of emergence of antagonism can never be eliminated. It is therefore an illusion to believe in the advent of a society from which antagonism would have been eradicated. Antagonism, as Schmitt says, is an ever present possibility; the political belongs to our ontological condition.

Next to antagonism, the concept of hegemony is the key notion for addressing the question of 'the political'. To take account of 'the political' as the ever present possibility of antagonism requires coming to terms with the lack of a final ground and acknowledging the dimension of undecidability which pervades every order. It requires in other words recognizing the hegemonic nature of every kind of social order and the fact that every society is the product of a series of practices attempting to establish order in a context of contingency. As Ernesto Laclau indicates, 'The two central features of a hegemonic intervention are, in this sense, the "contingent" character of the hegemonic articulations and their "constitutive" character, in the sense that they institute social relations in a primary sense, not depending on any a priori social rationality.'[8] The political is linked to the acts of hegemonic institution. It is in this sense that one has to differentiate the social from the political. The social is the realm of sedimented practices, that is, practices that conceal the originary acts of their contingent political institution and which are taken for granted, as if they were self-grounded. Sedimented social practices are a constitutive part of any possible society; not all social bonds are put into question at the same time. The social and the political have thus the status of what Heidegger called *existentials*, i.e. necessary dimensions of any societal life. If the political – understood in its hegemonic sense – involves the visibility of the acts of social institution, it is impossible to determine a priori what is social and what is political independently of any contextual reference. Society is not to be seen as the unfolding of a logic exterior to itself, whatever the source of this logic could be: forces of production, development of what Hegel called the Absolute Spirit, laws of history, etc. Every order is the temporary and precarious articulation of contingent practices. The frontier between the social and the political is essentially unstable and requires constant displacements and renegotiations between social agents. Things could always be otherwise and therefore every order is predicated on the exclusion of other possibilities. It is in that sense that it can be called 'political' since it is the expression of a particular structure of power relations. Power is constitutive of the social because the social could not exist without the power relations through which it is given shape. What is at a given moment considered as the 'natural' order – jointly with the 'common sense' which accompanies it – is the result of sedimented practices; it is never the manifestation of a deeper objectivity exterior to the practices that bring it into being.

To summarize this point: every order is political and based on some form of exclusion. There are always other possibilities that have been repressed and that can be reactivated. The articulatory practices through which a certain order is established and the meaning of social institutions is fixed are 'hegemonic pratices'. Every hegemonic order is susceptible of being challenged by counter-hegemonic practices, i.e. practices which will attempt to disarticulate the existing order so as to install another form of hegemony.

As far as collective identities are concerned, we find ourselves in a similar situation. We have already seen that identities are in fact the result of processes of identifications and that they can never be completely fixed. We are never confronted with 'we/they' oppositions expressing essentialist identities pre-existing the process of identification. Moreover since, as I have stressed, the 'they' represents the condition of possibility of the 'we', its 'constitutive outside', this means that the constitution of a specific 'we' always depends on the type of 'they' from which it is differentiated. This is a crucial point because it allows us to envisage the possibility of different types of we/they relation according to the way the 'they' is constructed.

I want to emphasize those theoretical points because they constitute the necessary framework for the alternative approach to democratic politics that I am advocating. To postulate the ineradicability of antagonism, while affirming at the same time the possibility of democratic pluralism, one has to argue *contra* Schmitt that those two assertions do not negate each other. The crucial point here is to show how antagonism can be transformed so at to make available a form of we/they opposition compatible with pluralist democracy. Without such a possibility one is left with the following alternatives: believing either with Schmitt in the contradictory nature of liberal democracy or with the liberals in the elimination of the adversarial model as a step forward for democracy. In the first case you acknowledge the political but foreclose the possibility of a pluralist democratic order, in the second case you postulate a completely unadequate, anti-political view of liberal democracy, the negative consequences of which we will consider in the following chapters.

WHICH WE/THEY FOR DEMOCRATIC POLITICS?

According to the previous analysis, it appears that one of the main tasks for democratic politics consists in defusing the potential antagonism that exists in social relations. If we accept that this cannot be done by transcending the we/they relation, but only by constructing it in a different way, then the following question arises: what could constitute a 'tamed' relation of antagonism, what form of we/they would it imply?

Conflict, in order to be accepted as legitimate, needs to take a form that does not destroy the political association. This means that some kind of common bond must exist between the parties in conflict, so that they will not treat their opponents as enemies to be eradicated, seeing their demands as illegitimate, which is precisely what happens with the antagonistic friend/enemy relation. However, the opponents cannot be seen simply as competitors whose interests can be dealt with through mere negotiation, or reconciled through deliberation, because in that case the antagonistic element would simply have been eliminated. If we want to acknowledge on one side the permanence of the antagonistic dimension of the conflict, while on the other side allowing for the possibility of its 'taming', we need to envisage a third type of relation. This is the type of relation which I have proposed to call 'agonism'.[9] While antagonism is a we/they relation in which the two sides are enemies who do not share any common ground, agonism is a we/they relation where the conflicting parties, although acknowledging that there is no rational solution to their conflict, nevertheless recognize the legitimacy of their opponents. They are 'adversaries' not enemies. This means that, while in conflict, they see themselves as belonging to the same political association, as sharing a common symbolic space within which the conflict takes place. We could say that the task of democracy is to transform antagonism into agonism.

This is why 'the adversary' is a crucial category for democratic politics. The adversarial model has to be seen as constitutive of democracy because it allows democratic politics to transform antagonism into agonism. In other words, it help us to envisage how the dimension of antagonism can be 'tamed', thanks to the establishment of institutions and practices through which the potential antagonism can be played out in an agonistic way. As I will argue at several points in this book, antagonistic conflicts are less likely to emerge as long as agonistic legitimate political channels for dissenting voices exist. Otherwise dissent tends to take violent forms, and this is true in both domestic and international politics.

I would like to stress that the notion of the 'adversary' that I am introducing needs to be distinguished sharply from the understanding of that term that we find in liberal discourse because in my understanding the presence of antagonism is not eliminated but 'sublimated' so to speak. For the liberals an adversary is simply a competitor. The field of politics is for them a neutral terrain in which different groups compete to occupy the positions of power; their objective is merely to dislodge others in order to occupy their place, They do not put into question the dominant hegemony and there is no attempt at profoundly transforming the relations of power. It is merely a competition among elites.

What is at stake in the agonistic struggle, on the contrary, is the very configuration of power relations around which a given society is structured: it is a struggle between opposing hegemonic projects which can never be reconciled rationally. The antagonistic dimension is always present, it is a real confrontation but one which is played out under conditions regulated by a set of democratic procedures accepted by the adversaries.

CANETTI ON THE PARLIAMENTARY SYSTEM

Elias Canetti is one of the authors who understood perfectly that the establishment of 'agonistic' relations was the task of democratic politics. In a few brilliant pages in *Crowds and Power* dedicated to analysing the nature of the parliamentary system, in the chapter 'The Crowd in History', Canetti indicates how such a system uses the psychological structure of opposing armies and stages a form of warfare which has renounced killing. According to him:

> A parliamentary vote does nothing but ascertain the relative strength of two groups at a given time and place. Knowing them beforehand is not enough. One party may have 360 members and the other only 240, but the actual vote is decisive, as the moment in which the one is really measured against the other. It is all that is left of the original lethal clash and it is played out in many forms, with threats, abuse and physical provocation which may lead to blows or missiles. But the counting of the vote ends the battle.[10]

And later he adds: 'The solemnity of all those activities derives from the renunciation of death as an instrument of decision. Every single vote puts death, as it were, on one side. But the effect that killing would have had on the strength of the enemy is scrupulously put down in figures; and any one who tampers with these figures, who destroys or falsifies them, lets death in again without knowing it.'[11]

This is an excellent example of how enemies can be transformed into adversaries, and we see here very clearly how, thanks to democratic institutions, conflicts can be staged in a way which is not antagonistic but agonistic. According to Canetti, modern democracy and the parliamentary system should not be envisaged as a stage in the evolution of humankind in which people, having become more rational, are now able to act rationally, either to promote their interests or to exercise their free public reason, as the aggregative and deliberative models would have it. And he stresses that:

parliaments

No one has ever really believed that the majority decision is necessarily the wiser one because it has received the greater number of votes. It is will against will as in war. Each is convinced that right and reason are on his side. Conviction comes easily and the purpose of the party is, precisely, to keep this will and conviction alive. The member of an outvoted party accepts the majority decision, not because he has ceased to believe in his own case, but simply because he admits defeat.[12]

I find Canetti's approach really illuminating. He makes us grasp the important part played by the parliamentary system in the transformation of antagonism into agonism and in the construction of a we/they compatible with democratic pluralism. When parliamentary institutions are destroyed or weakened, the possibility of an agonistic confrontation disappears and it is replaced by an antagonistic we/they. Think for instance of the case of Germany and the way in which, with the collapse of parliamentary politics, the Jews became an antagonistic 'they'. This, I think, is something worth meditating on for left-wing opponents of parliamentary democracy!

There is another aspect of Canetti's work, his reflections on the phenomenon of the 'crowd', which provides important insights for a critique of the rationalist perspective dominant in liberal political theory. Scrutinizing the permanent appeal exercised by the manifold types of crowds in all types of societies, he attributes it to the different drives which move social agents. On one side there is what one could describe as a drive towards individuality and distinctiveness. But there is another drive that makes them want to become part of a crowd to lose themselves in a moment of fusion with the masses. This attraction of the crowd is not for him something archaic and premodern, destined to disappear with the advances of modernity. It is part and parcel of the psychological make-up of human beings. The refusal to admit this tendency is what is at the origin of the rationalist approach's incapacity to come to terms with political mass movements, which they tend to see as an expression of irrational forces or a 'return of the archaic'. On the contrary, once we accept with Canetti that the 'crowd' appeal will always be with us, we have to approach democratic politics in a different way, addressing the issue of how it can be mobilized in ways which will not threaten democratic institutions.

What we are encountering here is the dimension of what I have proposed to call 'passions' to refer to the various affective forces which are at the origin of collective forms of identifications. By putting the accent either on the rational calculation of interests (aggregative model), or on moral deliberation (deliberative model), current democratic political theory is unable to acknowledge the role of 'passions' as one of the main moving forces in the field of politics and finds itself disarmed when faced with its diverse manifestations. Now, this chimes with the refusal to accept the ever present possibility of antagonism and the belief that, as far as it is rational, democratic politics can always be interpreted in terms of individual actions. Were this not possible, it must necessarily be due to backwardness. As we will see in the following chapter, this is, for instance, how the advocates of 'reflexive modernization' interpret any kind of disagreement with their theses.

Given the current emphasis on consensus, it is not surprising that people are less and less interested in politics and that the rate of abstention is growing. Mobilization requires politicization, but politicization cannot exist without the production of a conflictual representation of the world, with opposed camps with which people can identify, thereby allowing for passions to be mobilized politically within the spectrum of the democratic process. Take the case of voting for instance. What the rationalist approach is unable to grasp is that what moves people to vote is much more than simply the defence of their interests. There is an important affective dimension in voting and what is at stake there is a question of identification. In order to act politically people need to be able to identify with a collective identity which provides an idea of themselves they can valorize. Political discourse has to offer not only policies but also identities which can help people make sense of what they are experiencing as well as giving them hope for the future.

FREUD AND IDENTIFICATION

To take into account the affective dimension of politics is therefore crucial for democratic theory and this calls for a serious engagement with psychoanalysis. Freud's analysis of the process of 'identification' brings out the libidinal investment at work in the creation of collective identities and it gives important clues concerning the emergence of antagonisms. In *Civilization and Its Discontents*, he presents a view of society as perpetually threatened with disintegration because of the inclination to aggression present in human beings. According to him 'men are not gentle creatures who want to be loved, and who at the most can defend themselves if they are attacked; they are, on the contrary, creatures among whose instinctual endowments is to be reckoned a powerful share of aggressiveness.'[13] Civilization, in order to check those aggressive instincts, needs to use different methods. One of those consists in fostering communal bonds through the mobilization of the libidinal instincts of love. As he asserts in *Group Psychology and the Analysis of the Ego*, 'a group is clearly held together by a power of some kind: and to what power could this feat be better ascribed than to Eros, which holds together everything in the world'[14] The aim is to establish strong identifications between the members of the community, to bind them in a shared identity. A collective identity, a 'we', is the result of a libidinal investment, but this necessarily implies the determination of a 'they'. To be sure, Freud did not see all opposition as enmity, but he was aware that it could always become enmity. As he indicates, 'It is always possible to bind together a considerable amount of people in love, so long as there are other people left over to receive the manifestation of their aggressiveness.'[15] In such a case the we/they relation becomes one of enmity, i.e. it becomes antagonistic.

According to Freud, the evolution of civilization is charac-terized by a struggle between two basic types of libidinal instincts, Eros the instinct of life and Death the instinct of aggressiveness and destructiveness. He also stressed that 'the two kinds of instinct seldom – perhaps never – appear in isolation from each other, but are alloyed with each other in varying and very different proportions and so become unrecognizable to our judgment.'[16] The aggressive instinct can never be eliminated but one can try to disarm it, so to speak, and to weaken its destructive potential by several methods which Freud discusses in his book. What I want to suggest is that, understood in an agonistic way, democratic institutions can contribute to this disarming of the libidinal forces leading towards hostility which are always present in human societies.

Further insights can be gained from the work of Jacques Lacan, who developing Freud's theory, has introduced the

always take place through a we/they kind of differentiation, one can understand how nationalism can easily be transformed into enmity. For Žižek, nationalist hatred emerges when another nation is perceived as threatening our enjoyment. It has its origin therefore in the way social groups deal with their lack of enjoyment by attributing it to the presence of an enemy which is 'stealing' it. To envisage how such a transformation of national identifications into friend/enemy relations can be averted, it is necessary to acknowledge the affective bonds which support them. Now, this is precisely what the rationalist approach forecloses, hence the impotence of liberal theory in face of the eruption of nationalist antagonisms.

The lesson to be drawn from Freud and Canetti is that, even in societies which have become very individualistic, the need for collective identifications will never disappear since it is constitutive of the mode of existence of human beings. In the field of politics those identifications play a central role and the affective bond which they provide needs to be taken into account by democratic theorists. To believe that we have entered into an age where 'post-conventional' identities make possible a rational treatment of political questions, thereby eluding the role of a democratic mobilization of affects, is to abandon that terrain to those who want to undermine democracy. The theorists who want to eliminate passions from politics and argue that democratic politics should be understood only in terms of reason, moderation and consensus are showing their lack of understanding of the dynamics of the political. They do not see that democratic politics needs to have a real purchase on people's desires and fantasies and that, instead of opposing interests to sentiments and reason to passions, it should offer forms of identifications conducive to democratic practices. Politics has always a 'partisan' dimension and for people to be interested in politics they need to have the possibility of choosing between parties offering real alternatives. This is precisely what is missing in the current celebration of 'partisan-free' democracy. Despite what we hear in many quarters, the kind of consensual politics dominant today, far from representing a progress in democracy, is the sign that we live in what Jacques Rancière calls a 'post-democracy'. In his view the consensual practices which are today proposed as the model for democracy presuppose the very disappearance of what constitutes the vital core of democracy. As he says,

> Postdemocracy is the government practice and conceptual legitimation of a democracy after the demos, a democracy that has eliminated the appearance, miscount, and dispute of the people and is thereby reducible to the sole interplay of state mechanisms and combinations of social energies and interests. . . . It is the practice and theory of what is appropriate with no gap left between the forms of the state and the state of social relations.[20]

What Rancière points out here, albeit using a different vocabulary, is the erasure by the post-political approach of the adversarial dimension which is constitutive of the political and which provides democratic politics with its inherent dynamics.

AGONISTIC CONFRONTATION

Many liberal theorists refuse to acknowledge the antagonistic dimension of politics and the role of affects in the construction of political identities because they believe that it would endanger the realization of consensus, which they see as the aim of democracy. What they do not realize is that, far from jeopardizing democracy, agonistic confrontation is the very condition of its existence. Modern democracy's specificity lies in the recognition and legitimation of conflict and the refusal to suppress it by imposing an authoritarian order. Breaking with the symbolic representation of society as an organic body – characteristic of the holist mode of organization – a pluralist liberal democratic society does not deny the existence of conflicts but provides the institutions allowing them to be expressed in an adversarial form. It is for this reason that we should be very wary of the current tendency to celebrate a politics of consensus, claiming that it has replaced the supposedly old-fashioned adversarial politics of right and left. A well functioning democracy calls for a clash of legitimate democratic political positions. This is what the confrontation between left and right needs to be about. Such a confrontation should provide collective forms of identification strong enough to mobilize political passions. If this adversarial configuration is missing, passions cannot be given a democratic outlet and the agonistic dynamics of pluralism are hindered. The danger arises that the democratic confrontation will therefore be replaced by a confrontation between essentialist forms of identification or non-negotiable moral values. When political frontiers become blurred, disaffection with political parties sets in and one witnesses the growth of other types of collective identities, around nationalist, religious or ethnic forms of identification. Antagonisms can take many forms and it is illusory to believe that they could ever be eradicated. This is why it is important to allow them an agonistic form of expression through the pluralist democratic system.

Liberal theorists are unable to acknowledge not only the primary reality of strife in social life and the impossibility of finding rational, impartial solutions to political issues but also the integrative role that conflict plays in modern democracy. A democratic society requires a debate about possible alternatives and it must provide political forms of collective identification around clearly differentiated democratic positions. Consensus is no doubt necessary, but it must be accompanied by disssent. Consensus is needed on the institutions constitutive of democracy and on the 'ethico-political' values informing the political association – liberty and equality for all – but there will always be disagreement concerning their meaning and the way they should be implemented. In a pluralist democracy such disagreements are not only legitimate but also necessary. They provide the stuff of democratic politics.

Besides the shortcomings of the liberal approach, the main obstacle to the implementation of an agonistic politics comes from the fact that, since the collapse of the Soviet model, we are witnessing the unchallenged hegemony of neo-liberalism with its claim that there is no alternative to the existing order. This claim has been accepted by social democratic parties which, under the pretence of 'modernizing', have been steadily moving to the right, redefining themselves as 'centre-left'. Far from profiting from the crisis of its old communist antagonist, social democracy has been dragged into its collapse. In this way a great opportunity has been lost for democratic politics. The events of 1989 should have provided the time for a redefinition of the left, now liberated of the weight previously represented by the communist system. There was a real chance for a deepening of the democratic project because traditional political frontiers, having been shattered, could have been redrawn in a more progressive way. Unfortunately this chance has been missed. Instead we heard triumphalist claims about the disappearance of antagonism and the advent of a politics without frontiers, without a 'they'; a win-win politics in which solutions could be found favouring everybody in society.

While it was no doubt important for the left to come to terms with the importance of pluralism and liberal democratic political institutions, this should not have meant abandoning all attempts to transform the present hegemonic order and accepting the view that 'really existing liberal democratic societies' represent the end of history. If there is a lesson to be drawn from the failure of communism it is that the democratic struggle should not be envisaged in terms of friend/enemy and that liberal democracy is not the enemy to be destroyed. If we take 'liberty and equality for all' as the 'ethico-political' principles of liberal democracy (what Montesquieu defined as 'the passions that move a regime'), it is clear that the problem with our societies is not their proclaimed ideals but the fact that those ideals are not put into practice. So the task for the left is not to reject them, with the argument that they are a sham, a cover for capitalist domination, but to fight for their effective implementation. And this of course cannot be done without challenging the current neo-liberal mode of capitalist regulation.

This is why such a struggle, if it should not be envisaged in terms of friend/enemy, cannot be simply envisaged as a mere competition of interests or on the 'dialogic' mode. Now, this is precisely how most left-wing parties visualize democratic politics nowadays. To revitalize democracy, it is urgent to get out of this impasse. My claim is that, thanks to the idea of the 'adversary', the agonistic approach that I am proposing could contribute to a revitalization and deepening of democracy. It also offers the possibility of envisaging the left's perspective in an hegemonic way. Adversaries inscribe their confrontation within the democratic framework, but this framework is not seen as something immutable: it is susceptible of being redefined through hegemonic struggle. An agonistic conception of democracy acknowledges the contingent character of the hegemonic politico-economic articulations which determine the specific configuration of a society at a given moment. They are precarious and pragmatic constructions which can be disarticulated and transformed as a result of the agonistic struggle among the adversaries.

Slavoj Žižek is therefore mistaken to assert that the agonistic approach is unable to challenge the status quo and ends up accepting liberal democracy in its present stage.[21] What an agonistic approach certainly disavows is the possibility of an act of radical refoundation that would institute a new social order from scratch. But a number of very important socio-economic and political transformations, with radical implications, are possible within the context of liberal democratic institutions. What we understand by 'liberal democracy' is constituted by sedimented forms of power relations resulting from an ensemble of contingent hegemonic interventions. The fact that their contingent character is not recognized today is due to the absence of counter-hegemonic projects. But we should not fall again into the trap of believing that their transformation requires a total rejection of the liberal-democratic framework. There are many ways in which the democratic 'language-game' – to borrow a term from Wittgenstein – can be played, and the agonistic struggle should bring about new meanings and fields of application for the idea of democracy to be radicalized. This is, in my view, the effective way to challenge power relations, not on the mode of an abstract negation but in a properly hegemonic way, through a process of disarticulation of existing practices and creation of new discourses and institutions. Contrary to the various liberal models, the agonistic approach that I am advocating acknowledges that society is always politically instituted and never forgets that the terrain in which hegemonic interventions take place is always the outcome of previous hegemonic practices and that it is never a neutral one. This is why it denies the possibility of a non-adversarial democratic politics and criticizes those who, by ignoring the dimension of 'the political', reduce politics to a set of supposedly technical moves and neutral procedures.

Three

The post-political perspective that this book intends to challenge finds its sociological bearings in a picture of the world first elaborated by a variety of theorists who in the early 1960s announced the coming of a 'post-industrial society' and celebrated 'the end of ideology'. This tendency went later out of fashion but it has been revived in a new guise by sociologists such as Ulrich Beck and Anthony Giddens who argue that the model of politics structured around collective identities has become hopelessly outdated, owing to the growth of individualism, and that it needs to be relinquished. According to them we are now in a second stage of modernity which they call 'reflexive modernity'. Our societies have become 'post-traditional' and this calls for a drastic rethinking of the nature and aims of politics. Widely diffused in the media, those ideas are fast becoming the 'common sense' which informs the mainstream perception of our social reality. They have been influential in political circles and, as we will see, they have played a role in the evolution of several social democratic parties. Since they provide several central tenets of the current *Zeitgeist*, the objective of this chapter is to examine them closely and to scrutinize their consequences for democratic politics.

BECK AND THE 'REINVENTION OF POLITICS'

To assess critically Ulrich Beck's claim that politics needs to be 'reinvented', we need first to grasp the main lines of his theory of 'reflexive modernity' and his conception of 'risk society'. Those ideas have been elaborated in a series of books published since 1986 where he affirms that industrial societies have undergone crucial changes in their internal dynamics. His main argument is that after a first stage of 'simple modernization', characterized by the belief in the unlimited sustainability of natural techno-economic progress, whose risks could be contained thanks to adequate monitoring institutions, we now live in an epoch of 'reflexive modernization', characterized by the emergence of a 'risk society'. Modern societies are now confronted with the limits of their own model and the awareness that progress could turn into self-destruction if they are unable to control the side-effects of their inherent dynamism. We have become aware that certain features of industrial society are socially and politically problematic. It is now time to acknowledge that economic, social, political and individual risks confronting advanced industrial societies cannot be dealt with any more through traditional institutions.

According to Beck, one of the crucial difference between the first and the second modernity is that nowadays the motor of social history does not reside any more in instrumental rationality but in the 'side-effect'. He states, 'while simple modernization ultimately situates the motor of social change in categories of instrumental rationality (reflection), "reflexive" modernization conceptualizes the motive power of social change in categories of the side-effect (reflexivity). Things at first unseen and unreflected, but externalized, add up to structural rupture that separates industrial from "new modernities" in the present and the future.'[1] He puts great emphasis on the fact that this transition from one social epoch to another has taken place surreptitiously, in an unplanned way. It is not the result of political struggles and should not be interpreted according to the marxist idea of the revolution. Indeed, it is not the crises but the victories of capitalism which are at the origin of this new society which should be envisaged as the victory of Western modernization.

Here is an example of what he means by the role of 'side-effects': 'the transition from the industrial to the risk period of modernity occurs undesired, unseen and compulsively in the wake of the autonomized dynamism of modernization, following the pattern of latent side-effects'.[2] It is those side-effects, not political struggles, which are at the origin of the profound changes which have taken place in a wide range of social relations: classes, sex roles, family relations, work etc. As a consequence constitutive pillars of the first modernity such as the trade unions and the political parties have lost their centrality because they are not adapted to deal with the new forms of conflict specific to reflexive modernity. In a risk society the basic conflicts are no longer of a distributional nature, about income, jobs, welfare benefits, but are conflicts over 'distributive responsibility', i.e. how to prevent and control the risks accompanying the production of goods and the threats entailed by the advances of modernization.

The societies of the first modernity, says Beck, were characterized by the nation-state and the crucial role of collective groups. Owing to the consequences of globalization on one side and the intensification of the processes of individualization on the other, this is no longer the case. Collective identities have been deeply undermined, both in the private and in the public realm, and the basic institutions of society are now oriented towards the individual and no longer towards the group or the family. Moreover, industrial societies were centred on 'work' and organized towards full employment; the status of individuals was essentially defined by their job, which also constituted an important condition for their access to democratic rights. This has also come to an end. Hence the urgency of finding a new way of envisaging the basis for an active participation in society, taking in account the fact that individuals are constructed in an open-ended discursive interplay to which the classical roles of industrial society cannot do justice.

While acknowledging that the old vocabulary of left and right, the conflicting interests of groups and the political parties have not yet disappeared, Beck considers that they are conceptual 'crutches of the past' and that they are thoroughly inadequate to grasp the conflicts of reflexive modernity. In a risk society ideological and political conflicts can no longer be ordained through the left/right metaphor which was typical of industrial society but are better characterized by the following dichotomies: safe/unsafe, inside/outside and political/unpolitical.[3]

THE EMERGENCE OF 'SUB-POLITICS'

Now that we have broadly delineated the framework of Beck's theory, we can examine the new form of politics which he advocates as a solution and which he calls 'sub-politics'. The central idea is that in a risk society one should not look for the political in the traditional arenas such as parliament, political parties and trade unions and that it is necessary to stop the equation between politics and state or between politics and political system. Today the political erupts in very different places and we are confronted with a paradoxical situation:

'the political constellation of industrial society is becoming unpolitical, while what was unpolitical in industrialism is becoming politicals'.[4] A series of new resistances have emerged which are grass roots-oriented, extra-parliamentary and no longer linked to classes or to political parties. Their demands concern issues which cannot be expressed through traditional political ideologies and they are not addressed to the political system: they take place in a variety of sub-systems.

Beck claims that 'risk society' challenges the basic tenets of political science which has generally elaborated the concept of politics in three aspects: (1) the 'polity' which concerns the institutional constitution of the political community; (2) 'policy' which examines how political programmes can shape social circumstances; (3) 'politics' which deals with the process of political conflict over power-sharing and power positions. In all three cases the question is directed at collective agents and the individual is not fit for politics. With the advent of sub-politics, the individual is now put at the centre of the political scene. 'Sub-politics', he declares,

> is distinguished from 'politics' in that (a) agents outside the political or corporatist system are allowed also to appear on the stage of social design (this group includes professional and occupational groups, the technical intelligentsia in companies, research institutions and management, skilled workers, citizens' initiatives, the public sphere and so on), and (b) not only social and collective agents but individuals as well compete with the latter and each other for the emerging power to shape politics.[5]

He also stresses that sub-politics means 'shaping society from below' and that in the wake of sub-politicization, there are growing opportunities to have a voice and a share in the arrangement of society for groups hitherto uninvolved in the substantive technification and industrialization process: citizens, the public sphere, social movements, expert groups, working people on site.[6]

When it comes to visualizing the issues which this reinvented sub-politics will tackle, Beck underlines again the differences from the type of left/right politics of simple modernity with its sharp separation between public and private. According to the traditional conception, one had to leave the private sphere in order to become political and it was only in the public sphere, through party politics, that the political was achieved. Sub-politics operates a reversal of this conception and puts at the centre of the political arena all the things which were left aside and excluded in the left/right axis. Now that all the questions which concern the self and which were perceived as expressions of individualism occupy centre stage, a new identity of the political emerges in terms of 'life-and-death politics'. In a risk society, which has become aware of the possibility of an ecological crisis, a series of issues which were previoulsy considered of a private character, such as those concerning the lifestyle and diet, have left the realm of the intimate and the private and have become politicized. The relation of the individual to nature is typical of this transformation since it is now inescapably interconnected with a multiplicity of global forces from which it is impossible to escape.

Moreover, technological progress and scientific developments in the field of medicine and genetic engineering are now forcing people to make decisions in the field of 'body politics' hitherto unimaginable. Those decisions on life and death are putting philosophical issues of existentialism on the political agenda and individuals will be obliged to confront them if they do not want their future to be left in the hands of experts or dealt with according to the logic of the market. Beck claims that this gives us the possibility of changing society in an existential sense. Everything depends on the capacity of people to shed their old modes of thought, inherited from the first modernity, so as to meet the challenges posed by risk society. The model of unambiguous intrumental rationality should be abolished and ways of making the 'new ambivalence' acceptable have to be found. What is needed is the creation of forums where a consensus could be built between the experts, the politicians, the industrialists and the citizens on ways of establishing possible forms of co-operation among them. This would require the transformation of expert systems into democratic public spheres.

Beck likes to stress the positive role that doubt can play in fomenting compromises which make the overcoming of conflicts possible. The generalization of an attitude of doubt, he claims, shows the way to a new modernity, based no longer on certainty like simple modernity but on the acknowledgement of ambivalence and the refusal of a superior authority. He asserts that the generalized scepticism and the centrality of doubt which are prevalent today preclude the emergence of antagonistic relations. We have entered an era of ambivalence in which nobody can believe any more that they possess the truth, belief which was precisely where antagonisms were stemming from. Therefore the very ground for their emergence has been eliminated.[7] This is why he dismisses attempts to speak in terms of left and right and to organize collective identities around those lines as 'crutches of the past'. He even goes so far as to assert that 'the political programme of a radicalized modernization is scepticism'.

In Beck's view, a society where doubt has been generalized will be unable to think in terms of friend and enemy, and a pacification of conflicts will follow. He takes it for granted that, once they stop believing in the existence of a truth that they can possess, people will realize that they have to be tolerant of other viewpoints and he believes that they will make compromises instead of trying to impose their own ideas. Only those who still think according to the old categories and who are unable to put their dogmatic certainties into question will still behave in an adversarial manner. Hopefully, the side-effects of reflexive modernization will lead to their disappearance and we can therefore reasonably expect the advent of a cosmopolitan order.

GIDDENS AND THE POST-TRADITIONAL SOCIETY

In the case of Anthony Giddens the key concept is 'post-traditional society'. What he wants to indicate by this concept is that we are caught up in everyday experiments which have profound consequences for the self and identity and which involve a multiplicity of changes and adaptation in daily life. Modernity has become experimental at a global level and it is fraught with global hazards whose outcome we cannot control: 'manufactured uncertainty' has become part of our life. Like Beck, Giddens believes that many of those uncertainties have been created by the very growth of human knowledge. They are the result of human intervention in social life and into nature. The growth of manufactured uncertainty has been accelerated by the intensifying of globalization thanks to the emergence of means of instantaneous global communication. The development of a globalizing cosmpolitan society has meant that traditions have become opened to interrogation, their status has changed because now justifications have to be offered for them and they can no longer be taken for granted as in the past.

The rise of a post-traditional social order has been accompanied by the expansion of 'social reflexivity' because manufactured uncertainty now intrudes into all areas of social life. Individuals have therefore to process a lot of information on which they need to act in their everyday actions. Giddens affirms that the development of social reflexivity is in fact the key to understanding a diversity of changes which have taken place both in economy and in politics. For instance 'the emergence of "post-Fordism" in industrial enterprises is usually analysed in terms of technological changes – particularly the influence of information technology. But the underlying reason for the growth of "flexible production" and "bottom-up decision-making" is that a universe of high reflexivity leads to greater autonomy of action, which the enterprise must recognize and draw on.'[8] A similar argument, he says, could be made in the sphere of politics concerning bureaucratic authority, which in his view is no longer a required condition for organizational effectiveness. This is why bureaucratic systems start to disappear and states can no longer treat their citizens as 'subjects'.

Giddens argues that we should now think in terms of 'life politics', which he opposes to the 'emancipative' mode. He asserts: 'Life politics concerns political issues which flow from processes of self-actualization in post-traditional contexts, where globalizing tendencies intrude deeply into the reflexive project of the self, and conversely where processes of self-realization influence global strategies.'[9] This means that 'life politics' includes for instance ecological questions and also the changing nature of work, the family, and personal and cultural identity. While emancipatory politics concerns life chances and freedom from different types of constraints, life politics concerns life decisions – decisions about how we should live in a post-traditional world where what used to be natural or traditional has now become opened to choice. It is not only a politics of the personal and it would be a mistake, stresses Giddens, to think that it is only a concern of the more affluent. To be sure ecological and feminist issues play a central role but life politics also covers more traditional areas of political involvement such as work and economic activity. It is therefore very relevant to tackle the manifold problems arising from the transformation of the labour force. His claim is that 'Life politics is about the challenges that face collective humanity'.[10]

Giddens joins Beck in underlining the growth of a new individualism which represents a real challenge to the usual ways of doing politics. In his view, this new individualism should be understood in the context of the complex effects of globalization and their impact in the diminishing role that tradition and customs play in our lives. Contrary to many left-wing as well as conservative critics, who see it as an expression of moral decay and as a threat to social solidarity, he sees institutional individualism as opening many positive possibilities, for instance as allowing a more adequate balance between individual and collective responsibilities. Indeed the fact that we are now living in a more reflective manner creates pressures towards greater democratization and this new individualism contributes in a crucial way to this democratic trend.[11]

DEMOCRATIZING DEMOCRACY

As we might expect from the previous considerations, Giddens sees the left/right divide as being obsolete. One of his books is even called *Beyond Left and Right*. He argues that with the demise of the socialist model and the fact that there is no longer an alternative to capitalism, the main dividing line between left and right has disappeared and that most of the new problems arising in the context of the post-traditional society, i.e. all those issues concerning 'life politics', cannot be expressed within the left/right framework. A detradition-alizing social order requires a new type of 'generative politics' according to which: (1) the desired outcomes are not deter-mined from the top; (2) situations are created in which active trust can be built and sustained; (3) autonomy is granted to those affected by specific programmes or policies; (4) resources are generated which enhance autonomy, including material wealth; (5) political power is decentralized.[12]

Modern trust was invested mainly in expert-systems, but now says Giddens, what we need is 'active trust'. In a post-traditional context where the institutions have become reflex-ive, the propositions of experts are opened to critique by the citizens and passive trust is not enough, trust must become active. To generate active trust expert knowledge must be democratically validated. Indeed, scientific statements are now treated by the public as contestable propositional truths and this is why expert systems need to become dialogical. Hence his call for a 'dialogic democracy'. What is at stake is the creation of active trust generating social solidarity among individuals and groups. Active trust implies a reflexive engagement of lay people with expert systems instead of their reliance on expert authority.

In an argument akin to the one made by Beck about the need to transform expert systems in democratic public spheres, Giddens argues for the necessity of democratizing the main institutions of society (including the family) by opening them to debate and contestation. The aim is to promote the value of autonomy in the widest possible range of social relations and this requires the establishment of small-scale public spheres where conflicts of interests could be resolved through public dialogue. He points out that such a process of democratization is driven by the expansion of social reflexivity and detraditionalization and that it is already at work in at least four social contexts: (1) in the realm of personal life where, in sexual relations, parent–child relations and friendship, we are witnessing the emergence of an 'emotional democracy'; (2) in the organizational arena where bureaucratic hierarchies are being replaced by more flexible and decentralized sytems of authority; (3) in the development of social movements and self-help groups, where challenging different forms of authority and opening up spaces for public dialogue represents another potential for democratization; (4) at the global level, where democratizing tendencies drawing on a mixture of reflexivity, autonomy and dialogue may eventually generate a cosmopolitan global order.[13]

To be sure, Giddens does not exclude the possibility of setbacks and he acknowledges that the reassertion of traditional relations may breed fundamentalism and violence, but he is basically optimistic about the future of post-traditional societies. He emphasizes the fact that, in reflexive modernity, traditions are forced to justify themselves and that only those which are made available to discursive justification will be able to persist. Moreover, this requisite of discursive justification creates conditions for a dialogue with other traditions as well as with alternative modes of behaviour. One can therefore expect the growing availability of a 'dialogic democracy' where one is ready to listen and to debate with the other, and this both on the level of personal life and on that of the global order.

The opening out of science is central to the project of

dialogical democratization because, as in the field of 'emotional democracy', visibility and openness to public discussion are the preconditions for the advance of social reflexivity and the granting of autonomy. Giddens suggests that we should visualize dialogic democracy as linked to the development of what he calls 'pure relationship', i.e. a relationship into which one enters and remains for its own sake because of the rewards that associating with others brings. This type of pure relationship is found in the area of personal life and it is linked to the growth of 'emotional democracy' which he sees as the model for his dialogic approach. Indeed, there is according to Giddens a close link between pure relationship and dialogic democracy. Referring to the literature of marital and sexual therapy, he suggests that there are important parallels between the way they envisage the qualities required for a good relationship and the formal mechanisms of political democracy because in both cases the issue is of one of autonomy.[14]

Giddens summarizes his view in the following way:

Pressures towards democratization – which always face contrary influences – are created by the twin processes of globalization and institutional reflexivity. Detraditionalization disembeds local contexts of action and at the same time alters the character of the global order: even when they remain firmly adhered to, traditions are increasingly forced into contact with one another. Globalization, reflexivity and detraditionalization creates 'dialogic spaces' that must in some way be filled. These are spaces which can be engaged with dialogically, invoking mechanisms of active trust – but which can also be occupied by fundamentalisms.[15]

A POST-POLITICAL VISION

As should be clear by now, what the approach advocated by Beck and Giddens aims at eliminating from politics is the notion of the 'adversary', which, in Chapter 2 I have presented as the central one for democratic politics. Both of them believe that in the current stage of reflexive modernity a 'democratization of democracy' can take place without having to define an adversary. The main political questions nowadays concern issues about adjudication between different lifestyle claims, about the extension of autonomy to all the spheres where dialogic democratization can be implemented in order to foster the development of reflexivity. They need to be decided by individuals not groups and framed in terms of 'life politics' (Giddens) and 'sub-politics' (Beck). The democratic debate is envisaged as a dialogue between individuals whose aim is to create new solidarities and extend the bases of active trust. Conflicts can be pacified thanks to the 'opening up' of a variety of public spheres where, through dialogue, people with very different interests will make decisions about the variety of issues which affect them and develop a relation of mutual tolerance allowing them to live together. Disagreements will of course exist but they should not take an adversarial form.

Their main argument is that, in post-traditional societies, we no longer find collective identities constructed in terms of we/they, which means that political frontiers have dissipated. Collective and group-specific sources of meaning are suffering from exhaustion and individuals are now expected to live with a broad variety of global and personal risks without the old certainties. With the advent of risk society and the individualization of political conflicts, the old lines of conflict and partisan controversies have lost their relevance and the past obviously they cannot be allowed to participate in the dialogical discussion. In fact, if we accept the distinction which I have proposed between 'enemy' and 'adversary', this type of opponent is not an adversary but an enemy, i.e. one whose demands are not recognized as legitimate and who must be excluded from the democratic debate.

Several crucial consequences follow from the erasure of the place of the adversary and in the following chapter I will argue that it sheds light on the antagonistic form taken by some current political struggles. At this point what is important to stress is that, by declaring the end of the adversarial model of politics, the Beck/Giddens approach forecloses the possibility of giving an 'agonistic' form to political conflicts; the only possible form of opposition is the 'antagonistic' one. Indeed, if we accept to envisage the domain of politics according to their framework, we end up with the following picture: on one side, a mutiplicity of 'sub-political' struggles about a variety of 'life issues' which can be dealt with through dialogue; on the other side, either the old-fashioned 'traditionalists' or, more worryingly, the 'fundamentalists' fighting a backward struggle against the forces of progress.

Beck and Giddens are of course convinced that the 'forces of progress' will prevail and that a cosmopolitan order will be established, but how will we get there and what will happen in the meantime? How are we going, for instance, to address the profound inequalities which exist today in the world? It is noteworthy that neither Beck nor Giddens has much to say about power relations and the way they structure our societies. They emphasize social fluidity and completely ignore the way in which 'reflexive modernity' has seen the emergence of a new class whose power will have to be challenged if the basic institutions of the 'post-traditional' society are to allegiance to the basic principles of pluralist democracy. But that does not mean that any kind of adversarial confrontation is thereby foreclosed and that we are bound to endorse a consensual, dialogic approach. As I have argued in Chapter 2, the fundamental question for democratic theory is to envisage how the antagonistic dimension – which is constitutive of the political – can be given a form of expression that will not destroy the political association. I suggested that it required distinguishing between the categories of 'antagonism' (relations between enemies) and 'agonism' (relations between adversaries) and envisaging a sort of 'conflictual consensus' providing a common symbolic space among opponents who are considered as 'legitimate enemies'. Contrary to the dialogic approach, the democratic debate is conceived as a real confrontation. Adversaries do fight – even fiercely – but according to a shared set of rules, and their positions, despite being ultimately irreconcilable, are accepted as legitimate perspectives. The fundamental difference between the 'dialogical' and the 'agonistic' perspectives is that the aim of the latter is a profound transformation of the existing power relations and the establishment of a new hegemony. This is why it can properly be called 'radical'. To be sure, it is not the revolutionary politics of the jacobin type, but neither is it the liberal one of competing interests within a neutral terrain or the discursive formation of a democratic consensus.

Such an understanding of the 'adversary' is precisely what the Beck/Giddens approach is unable to visualize and this is why they remain squarely within the traditional parameters of liberal politics. Their 'democratizing of democracy' should therefore not be confounded with the 'radical democracy' that Ernesto Laclau and I advocated as early as 1985 in *Hegemony and Socialist Strategy*.[18] It is in fact worth spelling out the differences between the two perspectives, particularly since, at first sight, there might seem to exist many similarities. For instance, our book is also a critique of the jacobin model of politics and we acknowledge that politics is now taking place in a multiplicity of domains hitherto considered as non-political. One of the central theses of *Hegemony and Socialist Strategy* is the need to take account of all the democratic struggles which have emerged in a variety of social relations and which, we argued, could not be apprehended through the category of 'class'. Those struggles, usually designated as the 'new social movements', constitute the field of what Beck calls 'sub-politics' and Giddens 'life political issues'. There is therefore agreement on the importance of enlarging the domain of politics. But our perspectives diverge concerning the way political struggle should be envisaged. For us the radicalization of democracy requires the transformation of the existing power structures and the construction of a new hegemony. In our view, the building of a new hegemony implies the creation of a 'chain of equivalence' among the diversity of democratic struggles, old and new, in order to form a 'collective will', a 'we' of the radical democratic forces. This can be done only by the determination of a 'they', the adversary that has to be defeated in order to make the new hegemony possible. While keeping our distance from the leninist tradition of total revolutionary break, and stressing that our understanding of radical democracy was compatible with the maintenance of the institutions of the so-called 'formal democracy', we nevertheless also parted company with the liberal approach of the neutrality of the state. Despite its shortcomings, we see the marxist tradition as having made an important contribution to our understanding of the dynamics of the capitalist system and its consequences over world and those who still cling desperately to the past. To use 'modernization' in such a way is no doubt a powerful rhetorical gesture which allows them to draw a political frontier between 'the moderns' and 'the traditionalists or fundamentalists', while at the same time denying the political character of their move. Despite their thesis about the disappearance of the we/they distinction and its centrality in politics, it is not surprising that neither Beck nor Giddens can avoid establishing a frontier between we and they. This was to be expected, since such a frontier, as we have seen earlier, is constitutive of politics. But by presenting it, in a supposedly neutral way, as sociological evidence, they deny its political nature.

Such a denial constitutes the typical post-political gesture and it repays close examination which will bring us important insights. As we have just seen, while announcing the end of the adversarial model, Beck and Giddens cannot escape defining an adversary or enemy, who is the 'fundamentalist' opposing the process of reflexive modernization. So the 'we' of the 'modern people', i.e. those who are part of the movement of reflexive modernization, is constructed by the determination of a 'they', the traditionalists or fundamentalists who oppose this movement. They cannot take part in the dialogic process, whose borders are in fact constituted by their very exclusion. What is this, if not a typical friend/ enemy discrimination, but one which, as I have indicated, is not recognized as such because it is presented as a sociological fact and not as a political, partisan gesture?

What should we conclude from this? It means that, contrary to their claims, the political in its antagonistic dimension has not disappeared, but in this case it manifests itself under a different guise, as a mechanism of exclusion justified on pseudo-scientific grounds. What is really problematic from a political point of view is that such a mode of drawing the political frontier is not conducive to a vibrant democratic debate. When an exclusion is justified in this way, it is not open to political contestation and it is shielded from democratic discussion. Demands which are presented as coming from the traditionalists or fundamentalists can thereby be ignored in good conscience by 'dialogical' democrats.

In the next chapter, when I discuss the political consequences of the denial of the constitutive nature of antagonism, I will have the opportunity of giving other examples of the post-political legerdemain, which consists in drawing a political frontier while denying its political character. But before we reach this point, I want to examine the attempt to link the theses of 'reflexive modernity' to the concrete political strategy of the so-called 'radical centre'.

GIDDENS AND THE THIRD WAY

The main player in this field is Giddens, who is usually credited with the attempt to lay the intellectual foundations for the centre-left position referred to as 'the third way'. In two books, The Third Way and The Third Way and Its Critics, published respectively in 1998 and 2000, he tried to draw the consequences of his sociological theory for practical politics and made a series of proposals for the 'redefinition of social democracy after the death of socialism'. Scrutinising these will provide us with a privileged standpoint to test the impact of the post-political approach in the practice of politics.

Social democracy, asserts Giddens, must come to terms with the end of the bipolar world system and the demise of the communist model. In his view, the identity of social democrats has been thrown into crisis by the collapse of communism because, although they defined themselves in opposition to communism, they shared some of its perspectives. The time has therefore come for a radical rethinking. This, he says, requires facing five dilemmas: (1) the implications of globalization; (2) the consequences of the spread of individualism; (3) the loss of meaning of the left/right divide; (4) the fact that politics is taking place outside the orthodox mechanisms of democracy; (5) the need to take account of the ecological problems.[19]

The background of his thesis is that, under the present conditions of globalization, the Keynesian form of economic management, which was a cornerstore of social democracy, has been drastically weakened. Moreover, with the defeat of socialism as a theory of economic management, one of the main dividing lines between left and right has disappeared. Social democrats must acknowledge that there is no alternative to capitalism. Drawing on his theory of reflexive modernization, Giddens criticizes classical social democracy for the centrality it attributes to the state in social and economic life and for its distrust of civil society. This makes it very badly prepared to grasp the nature of the new individualism, which it accuses of destroying common values and public concerns. Viewing the growth of individualization processes with suspicion, social democrats miss the potential for greater democratization which those processes entail. They cling to the traditional institutions of the welfare state without realizing that the concept of collective provision has to be rethought and that, since we now live in a more open and reflective manner, a new balance between individual and collective responsibility has to be found.

According to Giddens, 'The overall aim of third way politics should be to help citizens pilot their way through the major revolutions of our time: *globalization, transformations in personal life* and our *relationship to nature*'.[20] He extols a positive attitude towards globalization, but envisaged as a wide phenomenon, not merely as a global market. Endorsing free trade, he recommends checking its destructive consequences by a concern with social justice. Finally, he declares that collectivism has to be relinquished and that expanding individualism needs to be accompanied by an extension of individual obligations. What is at stake is the establishment of a new relationship between the individual and the community whose motto could be 'no rights without responsibilities'. Another motto of third way politics is 'no authority without democracy'. In a post-traditional society, he claims, democracy is the only route to the justification of authority and he puts great emphasis on the creation of active trust as the way to maintain social cohesion and sustain social solidarity in contexts of reflexive modernization.

To allow for a widening of democracy, argues Giddens, it is necessary to reform the state and government to make them act in partnership with civil society. The kind of reforms that he advocates include decentralization, expanding the role of the public sphere, fostering of administrative efficiency, new experiments with democracy beyond orthodox voting processes and increased intervention in the field of risk management. Third way politics aims in this way at the creation of a new democratic state which will act in close co-operation with civil society in the context of a new mixed economy, which Giddens describes in the following way: 'The new mixed economy looks instead for a synergy between public and private sectors, utilizing the dynamism of markets but with the public interest in mind. It involves a balance between regulation and deregulation, on the transnational as well as national and local levels; and a balance between the economic and the non-economic in the life of the society'.[21] The welfare state is not going to be abandoned but the relationship between risk and security should be shifted so as to create a society of 'responsible risks takers'. Similarly the meaning of redistribution should be shifted towards the 'redistribution of possibilities'.

Particularly relevant for my argument is Giddens's assertion that third way politics is 'one-nation politics' because it underlines the non-conflictual nature of his political project. This, of course, chimes with the central tenets of his socio-logical theory, which, as we have seen, erases the dimension of antagonism from the political. In post-traditional societies disagreements do exist, but they can be overcome through dialogue and education; they are not the expression of fun-damental conflicts and society is no longer marked by class division. Indeed it is the very concept of class that his 'life politics' intends to abolish and to replace by questions of 'lifestyle'.

It is also worth underlining that Giddens designates this new democratic state as 'the state without enemies' and much of his argument is based on the idea that, with the passing of the bipolar era, states now face not enemies but dangers; hence the need to look for other sources of legitimacy than the ones provided by the threat of war. Those considerations were of course published before the events of 11 September 2001 and today, with the unleashing of the 'war against ter-rorism', they seem hopelessly outdated. I reckon, however, that Giddens might want to stick to his position, explaining those events as temporary setbacks provoked by the reactions of the fundamentalists to the advances of reflexive modernization.

How should we evaluate Giddens's political proposals? He claims that his aim is to contribute to a renewal of social democracy, but it is clear that this supposed renewal consists in making the social democratic project basically resign itself to accepting the present stage of capitalism. This is a drastic move since the aim of social democracy has always been to confront the systemic problems of inequality and instability generated by capitalism. However, having decreed that there is no alternative, Giddens feels entitled to relinquish this supposedly outdated dimension. He simply overlooks the systemic connections existing between global market forces and the variety of problems – from exclusion to environmental risks – that his politics pretends to tackle. It is only on this condition that he can envisage a 'dialogical politics' transcending the adversarial model and able to produce solutions benefiting all sectors of society. Such a consensual, post-political perspective is characterized by a side-stepping of fundamental conflicts and by an evasion of any critical analysis of modern capitalism. This is why it is unable to challenge the hegemony of neo-liberalism.

NEW LABOUR'S 'RENEWAL' OF SOCIAL DEMOCRACY

We find a confirmation of this fit between neo-liberal hegemony and the 'third way' when we examine how Giddens's proposals for a renewed social democracy have informed the politics of New Labour. I do not intend to make a detailed analysis of the various policies of the Blair government: it will be enough to indicate its principal orientation. The question I want to ask is: how radical is the politics of this so-called 'radical centre' and what kind of consensus has it tried to implement? And the answer is really depressing. As Stuart Hall has pointed out,[22] instead of challenging the neo-liberal hegemony implemented by eighteen years of Thatcherite rule, New Labour has picked up where Thatcherism left off. Blair chose to adapt to the neo-liberal terrain, albeit in a distinctive way. His project has been to absorb social democracy into neo-liberalism. New Labour long-term strategy, says Hall, is 'the transformation of social democracy into a particular variant of free market neo-liberalism'. Some social democratic objectives, aiming for instance at a certain level of redistribution and improvements of public services, are present but they are subordinated to the neo-liberal agenda of setting the corporate economy free of the regulations which previous social democratic governments had installed to control capitalism. The welfare state has been 'modernized' by the introduction of internal markets and the spread of management techniques promoting the key 'entrepreneurial values' of efficiency, choice and selectivity. True, the state is not seen as the enemy as in the case of neo-liberalism, but its role has been completely transformed. It is no longer 'to support the less fortunate or powerful in a society which "naturally" produces huge inequalities of wealth, power and opportunity, but to help individuals themselves to provide for all their social needs – health, education, environmental, travel, housing, parenting, security in unemployment, pensions in old age, etc'.[23] This is how 'active government' is understood by New Labour.

John Gray, who also stresses the importance of neo-liberal ideology and the cult of the market in the intellectual formation of New Labour, argues that, in the field of privatizations, Blair went even further than Thatcher would have envisaged. He gives as examples the introduction of market forces into the justice system and the prison services and notes: 'Here the market was being inserted in core of the state itself – a move that in Thatcher's time only the right-wing think-thanks supported'.[24] Other policies in which he sees Blair going further than Thatcher include the deregulation of postal services and the injection of market forces into the National Health Service.

A very clear sign of New Labour renunciation of its left identity is that it has abandoned the struggle for equality. The slogan of the party has now become to provide 'choice'. Classes have disappeared and the key terms today are those of 'inclusion' and 'exclusion'. Society is viewed as basically composed of middle classes; the only exceptions are a small elite of the very rich on one side and those who are 'excluded' on the other. This view of the social structure provides the basis for the 'consensus at the centre' that New Labour is advocating. This of course chimes with the tenet that 'post-traditional' societies are no longer structured through unequal power relations. By redefining the structural inequalities systematically produced by the market in terms of 'exclusion', one can dispense with the structural analysis of their causes, thereby avoiding the fundamental question of which changes in power relations are needed to tackle them. It is only in that way that a 'modernized' social democracy can eschew the traditional identity of the left and situate itself 'beyond left and right'.

One of the ways advocated by Giddens to transcend the old left/right division consists in establishing partnerships between the state and civil society and this idea has been enthusiastically adopted by New Labour through 'public–private partnerships' (PPP) – with disastrous results for public services. There is no need to retell here the disastrous story of the railways. The failure of the attempt to entrust to private companies the running of such a vital part of the transport system has been so blatant that the state had to be brought back. However this does not seem to have diminished New

Labour's fervour for the PPP, which it still tries to impose in other areas. The PPP strategy is of course paradigmatic of the third way: neither state (left) nor private sector (right), but their supposed harmonious partnership, with the state putting up the money for investments and the entrepreneurs reaping the profits and of course with the citizens (consumers in New Labour parlance) suffering accordingly!

This is how a supposed renewal of social democracy has produced a 'social democratic variant of neo-liberalism' (Hall). The case of New Labour makes clear that the refusal to acknowledge that a society is always hegemonically constituted through a certain structure of power relations leads to accepting the existing hegemony and remaining trapped within its configuration of forces. This is the necessary outcome of a 'consensus at the centre' which pretends that the adversarial model has been overcome. Instead of being the terrain where an agonistic debate takes place between left and right policies, politics is reduced to 'spinning'. Since there is no fundamental difference between them, parties will try to sell their products by clever marketing with the help of advertising agencies. The consequence has been a growing disaffection with politics and a drastic fall in participation in elections. How long will it take before citizens completely lose faith in the democratic process?

Four

If we are to believe the optimistic picture put forward by the theorists of 'reflexive modernization' and the politicians of the 'third way', notwithstanding some rearguard resistance to progress, the basic trend nowadays is towards a unified and pacified world. However, this is far from being the case and their post-political vision has increasingly been contradicted from many quarters. To be sure, in recent decades the frontiers between left and right have become increasingly blurred. But instead of creating the conditions for a more mature democracy, what we have witnessed in many Western societies is a loss of legitimacy of democratic institutions. Moreover, as far as international politics is concerned, the end of the bipolar world order has led not to a more harmonious system but to the explosion of a multiplicity of new antagonisms. Even before the dramatic events of 11 September 2001 and the 'war on terrorism' that they unleashed, it was already clear that antagonisms, far from having disappeared, were manifesting themselves in new forms in both national and international contexts.

For instance, the shallowness of the post-political approach had already been revealed by the emergence in several European countries of right-wing populist parties whose success confounded liberal theorists and commentators alike. How could they explain that, contrary to their claims about the demise of collective identities, so many people in advanced societies could be attracted by parties appealing to supposedly 'archaic' forms of identifications such as 'the people'? Having celebrated the arrival of a new kind of non-partisan individualist voter, detached from traditional affiliations, who was rationally 'picking and choosing' among different party policies, how could dialogic theorists make sense of this sudden eruption of populist passions?

A first answer was to attribute this phenomenon to a context in which past atavisms had not yet been overcome. This is, for instance, how the success of the Freedom Party in Austria was interpreted. The accepted view was that Jörg Haider's appeal was due to the fact that Austria was a country that had not yet managed to come to terms with its nazi past. No need to worry, this was a special case and such a phenomenon could not reproduce itself in other countries.

However, the inadequacy of this facile explanation based on the 'remains of the past' was quickly revealed by the emergence of similar parties in many other countries with a very different history. It is obviously impossible to attribute the growing success of right-wing populist parties in Belgium, Denmark, Switzerland, the Netherlands, Norway, Italy and France (to list only the most important ones) to the absence in those countries of a critical relationship with their past. So liberal theorists looked for other explanations to fit their rationalist approach, insisting for instance on the role of uneducated, lower-class voters, susceptible to being attracted by demagogues. In vain, because sociological analyses clearly indicate that voters for populist parties can be found in all sectors of the electorate.

Do we have to conclude then that there is no common

explanation for this new kind of right-wing populism? I do not believe this to be the case and I am convinced that it is certainly not a coincidence that we have witnessed in recent years the unexpected rise of parties whose success is based on their populist rhetorics. But instead of looking for the causes in signs of 'backwardness', either in the history of the country or in the social status of the electorate, it is to the shortcomings of the main political parties that we have to turn our attention.

RIGHT-WING POPULISM

When we examine the state of democratic politics in all the countries where right-wing populism has made serious inroads, we find a striking similarity. Their growth has always taken place in circumstances where the differences between the traditional democratic parties have become much less significant than before. In some cases, as in Austria, this was due to a long period of coalition government; in others, as in France, to the move towards the centre of parties previously clearly situated at the left of the political spectrum. But in each case a consensus at the centre had been established, which did not allow voters to make of a real choice between significantly different policies. In countries where the electoral sytem did not discriminate against third parties, right-wing demagogues were therefore able to articulate the desire for an alternative to the stifling consensus.

The case of Austria is particularly interesting because it provides one of the earliest corroboration of my argument.[1] The consensus at the centre was established there soon after the end of the Second World War through the creation of a 'grand coalition' between the conservative People's Party (ÖVP) and the Socialist Party (SPÖ). They devised a form of co-operation thanks to which they were able to control the

the aim of the two main parties had been to exclude the FPÖ from participating in government. However, this is not my concern here. What I want to emphasize is that, contrary to the widespread view, it is certainly not the appeal to supposed nazi nostalgia which accounts for the dramatic rise of the FPÖ but the ability of Haider to construct a powerful pole of collective identification around the opposition between 'the people' and the 'consensus elites'. Indeed, this is precisely this 'anti-establishment' pole that the party was unable to sustain once it became part of the governing coalition.

The construction of a similar anti-establishment bloc explains the success of the Vlaams Blok (VB) in Belgium. The stronghold of the party is located in Antwerp, where a coalition between socialists and Christian democrats has monopolized political power for several decades. This has allowed the VB to present itself as the only real alternative to those that it opposes as 'corrupt elites'.[2] In this case the 'cordon sanitaire' established by the main parties to prevent the VB (recently renamed Vlaams Belang) from coming to power is still in place but the party has been going from strength to strength, becoming the second most important party in the whole of Flanders in the 2004 European elections, with 24.1 per cent.

As far as France is concerned, it is notable that the rise of the Front National started in the 1980s when, after Mitterrand's victory, the Socialist Party began to move towards the political centre, abandonning all pretence at offering an alternative to the existing hegemonic order. This allowed Jean-Marie Le Pen to claim that he was the only one to challenge the dominant consensus. The solutions he proposes are of course unacceptable but one cannot deny the political character of his discourse. At the 2002 presidential elections, which were notable for the fact that the two main candidates, Jacques Chirac and the announced disappearance of collective identities and the victory of individualism, the collective dimension could not be eliminated from politics. If they were not available through traditional parties, collective identities were likely to be provided in other forms. This is clearly what is happening with right-wing populist discourse, which is replacing the weakened left/right opposition by a new type of we/they constructed around an opposition between 'the people' and 'the establishment'. Contrary to those who believe that politics can be reduced to individual motivations, the new populists are well aware that politics always consists in the creation of a 'we' versus a 'they' and that it requires the creation of collective identities. Hence the powerful appeal of their discourse which offers collective forms of identification around 'the people'.

If we relate this to the other point I made concerning the importance of the affective dimension in politics and the need to mobilize passions through democratic channels, we can understand why the rationalist model of democratic politics, with its emphasis on dialogue and rational deliberation, is particularly vulnerable when confronted with a populist politics offering collective identifications with a high affective content like 'the people'. In a context where the dominant discourse proclaims that there is no alternative to the current neo-liberal form of globalization and that we should accept its dictats, it is not surprising that a growing number of people are listening to those who proclaim that alternatives do exist and that they will give back to the people the power to decide. When democratic politics has lost its capacity to mobilize people around distinct political projects and when it limits itself to securing the necessary conditions for the smooth working of the market, the conditions are ripe for political demagogues to articulate popular frustration.

For some time the case of Britain seemed to provide a counter-example to such an evolution; however the recent success of the Independence Party in the 2004 European elections suggests that things might be changing. It is of course too early to predict the fate of such a party, and the British electoral system certainly does facilitate the rise of third parties. But the dramatic surge in the share of the votes needs to be taken seriously. It is undeniable that all the conditions nowadays exist in Britain for a right-wing populist party to exploit the popular frustration. Since the move to the right of New Labour under the leadership of Tony Blair, many traditional Labour voters no longer feel represented by the party. The demands of an increasing proportion of the popular sectors have been left out of the political agenda and they could easily be articulated through a populist discourse by a skilful demagogue. This is what has already been happening in many European countries and we could easily witness a similar phenomenon in British politics.

It is high time to realize that, to a great extent, the success of right-wing populist parties comes from the fact that they articulate, albeit in a very problematic way, real democratic demands which are not taken into account by traditional parties. They also provide people with some form of hope, with the belief that things could be different. Of course it is an illusory hope, founded on false premises and unacceptable mechanisms of exclusion where xenophobia usually plays a central role. But when they are the only channels for the expression of political passions, their pretence to represent an alternative is very seductive. This is why I submit that the success of right-wing populist parties is the consequence of the lack of a vibrant democratic debate in our post-democracies. It proves that, far from benefiting democracy, the blurring of the left/right frontier is undermining it. Through the drawing of new political frontiers the terrain is being created for the emergence of collective identities whose nature is inimical to democratic treatment.

The response of traditional parties to the rise of right-wing populism has clearly contributed to exacerbating the problem. Instead of scrutinizing the political, social and economic causes of this new phenomenon, they have quickly dismissed its novelty by labelling it as 'extreme-right'. This move allowed them to evade the question of its specificity and its causes and to avoid examining whether the 'good democrats' did not have some responsibility for the popular rejection of the established political institutions. The explanation was already at hand: it was the 'brown plague' rearing its ugly head again and it called for all the democratic forces to unite in resisting the reappearance of this evil force. This is why moral condemnation and the setting up of a 'cordon sanitaire' have so often constituted the answer to the rise of right-wing populist movements.

POLITICS IN THE REGISTER OF MORALITY

This moralistic reaction brings to light another very important shortcoming of the post-political perspective. The lack of a political analysis was, of course, to be expected on several grounds. Given that the dominant view was that the adversarial model of politics had been overcome and that collective political identities did not fit in with the 'second modernity', the emergence of right-wing populism could be interpreted only as the return of some archaic forces. This is why the category of the 'extreme right' came very handy. Furthemore, given that the tenets of the dominant perspective did not allow presenting the confrontation with right-wing populist parties as a manifestation of the adversarial model of politics, those parties could not be envisaged in political terms, i.e. as adversaries to be fought politically. So it was very convenient to draw the frontier at the moral level between 'the good democrats' and the 'evil extreme right'.

Note that there was an added bonus in this move, which was to create the 'constitutive outside' necessary to secure the identity of the 'we' of the consensual forces. As I have stressed earlier, there is no consensus without exclusion, no 'we' without a 'they' and no politics is possible without the drawing of a frontier. So, some form of frontier was necessary in order to establish the identity of the 'good democrats'. The trick was done by designating the 'they' as the 'extreme right'. In a typical liberal legerdemain, a political 'we'/'they' discrimination could in this way be instituted at the same time that its political character was denied by presenting it as being of a moral nature. The identity of the good democrats could thereby be obtained by the exclusion of the evil extreme right, without putting in question the thesis that the adversarial model of politics has been overcome.

Another added bonus was that passions could be mobilized against what was designated as the 'extreme right', using the traditional repertoire of antifascist discourse. People were made to feel very good and very virtuous by simply participating in the denunciation of the 'evil forces'. Of course, this mobilization of passions was not acknowledged as such but perceived as the rational reaction of moral human beings wanting to defend universal values. In that way it was made congruent with the dominant rationalist perspective.

The reactions to the 2000 elections in Austria provide a telling example of this moralistic reaction to the rise of right-wing populisn. When a coalition government was established between the conservatives and the populists, the outcry in Europe was general and the other fourteen EU governments decided to impose diplomatic 'sanctions' on the Austrian government. In the name of the defence of European values and the struggle against racism and xenophobia – always easier to denounce in others than to fight at home – politicians of right and left joined forces to ostracize the new coalition before it had even done anything that could be deemed reprehensible. All the good democrats considered it their duty to condemn the coming to power of a party presented as 'neo-nazi'. Led by a militant press, very happy to have found a new devil to fight, an incredible campaign of demonization was launched, which very quickly included all the Austrians accused of not having been properly 'denazified'. The condemnation of racism and xenophobia in Austria become a useful way to guarantee the unity of the 'good democrats', who could thereby proclaim their allegiance to democratic values, while evading any critical examination of their own policies at home.

We should realize that a particularly perverse mechanism is at play in those moralistic reactions. This mechanism consists in securing one's goodness, through the condemnation of the evil in others. Denouncing others has always been a powerful and easy way to obtain a high idea of one's moral worth. It is a form of self-idealization very acutely examined by François Flahaut under the name of 'puritanism of good feeling', which he describes in the following way: 'holding forth about doing good, sympathizing with the victims, expressing indignation about the wickedness of others'.[3] According to him, in our utilitarian and rationalist age, this mode of self-idealization is what is left for people to escape from their own mediocrity, cast evil outside themselves and rediscover some form of heroism. This no doubt explains the increasing role played by the moralistic discourse in our post-political societies.

There is, in my view, a direct link between the weakening of the political frontier characteristic of the adversarial model and the 'moralization' of politics. By using the term 'moralization' in this context I do not mean, of course, that now people act in the field of politics in search of the common good, according to motives that would be more disinterested or impartial. What I want to indicate is that, instead of being constructed in political terms, the 'we'/'they' opposition constitutive of politics is now constructed according to moral categories of 'good' versus 'evil'.

What this change of vocabulary reveals is not, as some would have it, that politics has been replaced by morality but that politics is being played out *in the moral register*. It is in that sense that I am proposing to understand the 'moralization' of politics – to indicate not that politics has become more moral but that nowadays political antagonisms are being formulated in terms of moral categories. We are still faced with political friend/enemy discriminations but they are now expressed using the vocabulary of morality. To be sure, this has already been the case for some time in international politics and those in the United States have always been particularly fond of using moral vocabulary to denounce their political enemies. George W. Bush's crusade against the 'axis of evil' has indeed many antecedents. Just remember Ronald Reagan and his 'evil empire'. But what is new is that, as the reactions to right-wing populism reveal, this moralization of politics is now taking place also in European domestic politics. And in this field it is clearly a consequence of the consensual post-adversarial model advocated by all those – arguably well-meaning theorists – who have contributed to the establishment of the post-political perspective.

Far from creating the conditions for a more mature and consensual form of democracy, to proclaim the end of adversarial politics produces, then, exactly the opposite effect. When politics is played out in the register of morality, antagonisms cannot take an agonistic form. Indeed, when opponents are defined not in political but in moral terms, they cannot be envisaged as an 'adversary' but only as an 'enemy'. With the 'evil them' no agonistic debate is possible, they must be eradicated. Moreover as they are often considered as the expression of some kind of 'moral disease', one should not even try to provide an explanation for their emergence and success. This is why, as we have seen in the case of right-wing populism, moral condemnation replaces a proper political analysis and the answer is limited to the building of a 'cordon sanitaire' to quarantine the affected sectors.

There is some irony in the fact that the approach which claims that the friend/enemy model of politics has been superseded ends up creating the conditions for the revitalization of the antagonistic model of politics that it has declared obsolete. However, there is no denying that the post-political perspective, by hindering the creation of a vibrant agonistic public sphere, leads to envisaging the 'they' as 'moral', i.e. 'absolute enemies', thereby fostering the emergence of antagonisms, which can jeopardize democratic institutions.

TERRORISM AS CONSEQUENCE OF A UNIPOLAR WORLD

My aim so far has been to bring to the fore the consequences of the dominant post-political perspective for the internal workings of democratic politics. Now, I would like to turn my attention to the international arena in order to put my agonistic approach to the test of world politics. Can we draw from recent international events some lessons concerning the consequences of not acknowledging the dimension of the political? How can we make sense of the events of 11 September 2001 and the multiplication of terrorist attacks within the agonistic framework? What could a properly political approach tell us about the antagonisms which have emerged in the last few years? On all those questions, it is worth listening again to Carl Schmitt.

Let us first clarify an important issue. Some people have suggested that the strategy of the neo-conservatives who are behind George W. Bush's 'war against terrorism' is influenced by Schmitt's view of politics as friend/enemy discrimination. They claim that visualizing politics in such a way creates a dangerous polarization between the 'civilized world' and the 'enemies of freedom'. Bush's crusade is then presented as the direct consequence of implementing a Schmittian understanding of the political. To find a way out of this predicament, we are told, it is urgent to come back to a consensual model of politics; what our globalized world needs is the implementation of a cosmopolitan liberal approach.

There is, I believe, a profound misunderstanding at play in this rapprochement between Schmitt and the neo-conservatives. To be sure, Schmitt, as we have seen, repeatedly emphasized that the 'differentia specifica' of the political was the friend/enemy discrimination. But he always stressed that such a discrimination had to be drawn in a properly political way, not on the basis of economics or ethics. He would certainly not have condoned Bush's use of the moral category of 'evil' to designate his enemies and he would have rejected his messianic discourse about the American duty to bring freedom and democracy to the world.

In fact, far from justifying Bush's strategy, Schmitt's approach provides us with many insights to undermine its basic tenets. Debunking its moralistic discourse helps us to understand the rhetorical moves which allow the current US government to confiscate and monopolize the idea of civilization. Schmitt was very critical of liberal universalism with its pretence of offering the true and only legitimate political system. He criticized the liberals for using the concept of 'humanity' as an ideological weapon of imperialist expansion and he saw humanitarian ethics as a vehicle of economic imperialism. And he pointed out that

> When a state fights its political enemy in the name of humanity, it is not a war for the sake of humanity, but a war wherein a particular state seeks to usurp a universal concept against its military opponent. At the expense of its opponent, it tries to identify itself with humanity in the same way as one can misuse peace, justice, progress and civilization in order to claim these as one's own and to deny the same to the enemy.[4]

This, he thought, explained why wars waged in the name of humanity were particularly inhuman since all means were justified once the enemy had been presented as an outlaw of humanity. The drawing of the frontier between friend and enemy as between the 'civilized world' and its 'evil enemies' would have been seen by him as typical of the liberal universalism which, in the name of human rights, arrogated to itself the right and duty to impose its order on the rest of the world.

Schmitt argued that there was no inclusion without exclusion, no norm without an exception, and he persistently exposed liberalism's pretence of complete inclusiveness and its claim to be speaking in the name of 'humanity'. He recognized, however, the rhetorical force of this identification with humanity, used by liberalism to render illegitimate any opposition to its rule. As William Rasch indicates, this was for Schmitt the central mechanism at work in the establishment of Western hegemony and he could not help admiring how the American system had managed to gain global hegemony by equating his particular interests with moral norms that were universally binding with the result that 'to oppose American hegemony is to oppose the universally good and common interests of humanity'.[5]

Schmitt, however, also warned that any attempt to impose one single model worldwide would have dire consequences. He was acutely aware of the dangers entailed by the direction in which international affairs were evolving. After the Second World War he dedicated an important part of his reflections to the decline of the political in its modern form and the loss by the state of its monopoly of the political. This was linked, in his view, to the dissolution of the 'Jus Publicum Europaeum', the inter-state European law which for three centuries had managed to keep war within certain limits. He was concerned by the consequences of this loss of monopoly because he feared that the decline of the state was creating the conditions for a new form of politics which he referred to as 'inter-national civil war'. As long as the Jus Publicum Europaeum existed, limits were imposed to war, and hostility was not absolute; the enemy was not treated as a criminal and not seen as the last enemy of humankind. According to Schmitt, things began to change because of a convergence of various factors: the development of technological means of destruction, the liberal attempt to outlaw war and the reintroduction of the category of the 'just war' contributed to the emergence of a discriminatory conception of war. 'The discriminatory concept of the enemy as criminal and the attendant implication of *justa causa* run parallel to the intensification of the means of destruction and the disorientation of theaters of war. Intensification of the technical means of destruction opens the abyss of an equally destructive legal and moral discrimination.'[6] Once a war could be deemed 'illegal', all limits to hostility were eliminated and the opponent was declared criminal and inhuman: the enemy became the 'absolute enemy'.

In *Theory of the Partisan*, published in 1963, Schmitt presents the partisan as the product of the dissolution of the classical state order structured around the demarcation between what is political and what is not political. The appearance of partisans is linked to the fact that the limitations of hostility have been lifted. Having been deprived of all rights, partisans find their rights in hostility. Once the legitimity which served as guarantee for their right and legal protection has been negated, it is in hostility that partisans finds a meaning for their cause. And Schmitt concludes his book with this chilling warning:

> In a world where the protagonists rush into the abyss of total degradation before exterminating themselves physically, new types of absolute hostility are bound to emerge. Hostility will become so terrible that may be it will not even be possible any more to speak of enmity or hostility. Both will be outlawed and condemned in due form before the start of the operation of extermination. This operation will then be totally abstract and absolute . . . The negation of real hostility will in this way open the way to the work of extermination of an absolute hostility.[7]

Since 11 September 2001 Schmitt's reflections on the status of a 'post-statist politics' have become more relevant than ever. Indeed, they can help us grasp the conditions of emergence of new antagonisms. As Jean-François Kervégan has suggested,[8] they allow us to approach the question of terrorism in a very different way from the one currently accepted, i.e. as the work of isolated groups of fanatics. Taking our bearings from Schmitt, we can see terrorism as the product of a new configuration of the political which is characteristic of the type of world order being implemented around the hegemony of a single hyper-power.

Like Kervégan I think that Schmitt's insights about the dangers of a unipolar world order throw light on the phenomenon of terrorism. It is certainly the case that there is a correlation between the now unchallenged power of the USA and the proliferation of terrorist groups. Of course in no way do I want to pretend that this is the only explanation for terrorism, which is due to a multiplicity of factors. But it is undeniable that it tends to flourish in circumstances in which there are no legitimate political channels for the expression of grievances. It is therefore not a coincidence that since the end of the cold war, with the untrammelled imposition of a neo-liberal model of globalization under the dominance of the United States, we have witnessed a significant increase in terrorist attacks. Nowadays the possibility of maintaining socio-political models different from the Western ones has been drastically reduced since all international organizations are more or less directly under the control of Western powers led by the United States.

Even liberal theorists such as Richard Falk and Andrew Strauss – whose cosmopolitan proposals I will examine in the next chapter – acknowledge the link between terrorism and the present world order when they say:

> With the possibility of direct and formalized participation in the international system foreclosed, frustrated individuals

and groups (especially when their own governments are viewed as illegitimate and hostile) have been turning to various modes of civic resistance, both peaceful and violent. Global terrorism is at the violent end of this spectrum of transnational protest, and its apparent agenda may be mainly driven by religious, ideological and regional goals rather than by resistance directly linked to globalization. But its extremist alienation is partly, at the very least, an indirect result of globalizing impacts that may be transmuted in the political unconscious of those so afflicted into grievances associated with cultural injustices.[9]

The situation in the international arena is today in many respects similar to the one that I pointed out earlier in domestic politics: the absence of an effective pluralism entails the impossibility for antagonisms to find agonistic, i.e. legitimate, forms of expression. It is no wonder that, when they explode, those antagonims take extreme forms, putting into question the very basis of the existing order. The issue is once more the negation of the dimension of the political and the belief that the aim of politics – whether at the national or the international level – is to establish consensus on one single model, thereby foreclosing the possibility of legitimate dissent. The lack of political channels for challenging the hegemony of the neo-liberal model of globalization is, I contend, at the origin of the proliferation of discourses and practices of radical negation of the established order.

Seen from this angle, terrorism highlights the dangers implied in the delusions of the universalist globalist discourse which postulates that human progress requires the establish-ment of world unity based on the implentation of the Western model. It shatters the illusions of the universalist humanitarians that antagonisms could be eliminated thanks to a unification of the world that would be achieved by transcending the political, conflict and negativity.

THE UNIVERSALITY OF LIBERAL DEMOCRACY

I am convinced that facing the challenge posed by terrorism requires acknowledging the constitutive nature of pluralism and imagining the conditions for its implementation at the world level. This means breaking with the very deeply entrenched conviction in Western democracies that they are the embodiment of the 'best regime' and that they have the 'civilizing' mission of universalizing it. No small task indeed, since a great part of democratic theory is dedicated to proving the superiority of liberal democracy which is presented as the only just and legitimate regime, whose institutions would, in idealized conditions, be chosen by all rational individuals.

One of the most sophisticated defenders of the moral superiority and universal validity of liberal constitutional democracy is Jürgen Habermas, whose work I will use to illustrate this type of reasoning. Habermas's ambition since *Between Facts and Norms* has been to resolve a long-disputed issue concerning the nature of the Western constitutional state marked by the articulation of the rule of law and the defence of human rights with democracy understood as popular sovereignty. Liberals and democrats (or republicans) have always disagreed about which should have the priority – human rights or popular sovereignty. For liberals, following Locke, it is clear that private autonomy, guaranteed by human rights and the rule of law, was primary, while democrats (and republicans) argue, following Rousseau, that priority should be granted to political autonomy made possible by democratic self-legislation. While for liberals a legitimate government is one that protects individual liberty and human rights, for democrats the source of legitimacy lies in popular sovereignty.

For a rationalist like Habermas this unresolved competition is unacceptable and he ventured 'to demonstrate that there is a conceptual or internal relation, and not simply a historically contingent association between the rule of law and democracy'.[10] He claims to have brought the dispute to a close thanks to his discourse-theoretical approach by showing the co-originality of private and public autonomy. Without entering into the details of a complex argument, this is in a nutshell how he summarizes it:

> the desired internal relations between 'human rights' and 'popular sovereignty' consists in the fact that the requirement of legally institutionalizing self-legislation can be fulfilled only with the help of a code that simultaneously implies the guarantee of actionable individual liberties. By the same token, the equal distribution of these liberties (and their 'fair value') can in turn be satisfied only by a democratic procedure that grounds the supposition that the outcome of political opinion-and will-formation are reasonable. This shows how private and public autonomy reciprocally presuppose one another in such a way that neither one may claim primacy over the other.[11]

In trying to reconcile the two elements of liberal democracy, the aim of Habermas is no less than to establish the privileged rational nature of liberal democracy and consequently its universal validity. Clearly, if liberal constitutional democracy is such a remarkable rational achievement – the reconciliation of the rule of law and human rights with democratic participation – on what grounds could one 'rationally' object to its implementation? Every opposition is automatically perceived as a sign of irrationality and moral backwardness and as being illegitimate. The implication is obviously that all societies should adopt liberal democratic institutions which are the only legitimate way to organize human coexistence. This is corroborated by Habermas when, taking up again the question of co-originality, but this time from the point of view of the mode of political legitimation and putting the emphasis on the legal system, he asks: 'What basic rights must free and equal citizens mutually accord one another if they want to regulate their common life legitimately by means of positive law?'[12] His answer is, of course, that legitimacy can be obtained only through human rights which institutionalize the communicative conditions for a reasonable will formation.

Human rights, says Habermas, are 'Janus-faced', with a moral universal content but also with the form of legal rights; hence the need for them to be embodied in a legal order. According to him, 'human rights belong structurally to a positive and coercive legal order which founds actionable individual legal claims. To this extent, it is part of the meaning of human rights that they claim the status of basic rights which are implemented within the context of some existing legal order.'[13] He recognizes that this creates a particular tension between their universal moral meaning and their local conditions of realization since so far they have achieved a positive form only within national legal orders of the democratic states. But he is convinced that their global institutionalization is well under way and that the worldwide acceptance of a system of cosmopolitan law is only a question of time.

Such a conviction is based on Habermas's belief that human rights are the answer given in the West to specific challenges posed by social modernity. He argues that, since all societies are now facing the same challenges, they are bound to adopt Western standards of legitimacy and legal systems based on human rights, independently of their cultural backgrounds. He is adamant that they provide the only acceptable basis of legitimation and that, whatever their origin, 'human rights confront us today with fact that leaves us no choice'.[14] It is at the socio-economic level that the alternatives lie, not at the cultural one, and he declares peremptorily:

> Asiatic societies cannot participate in capitalistic modernization without taking advantage of the achievements of an individualistic legal order. One cannot desire the one and reject the other. From the perspective of Asian countries, the question is not whether human rights, as part of an individualistic legal order, are compatible with the transmission of one's own culture. Rather, the question is whether the traditional forms of political and societal integration can be asserted against – or must instead be adapted to – the hard-to-resist imperatives of an economic modernization.[15]

There is no alternative to Westernization and, as William Rasch, commenting on this passage, points out, for Habermas 'despite his emphasis on procedure and the universality of his so-called "discourse principle", the choice that confronts "Asiatic societies" or any other people is a choice between cultural identity and economic survival, between in other words, cultural and physical extermination'.[16]

If such is the alternative for non-Western societies, should we be suprised to witness the emergence of violent resistance? It is high time to wake up from the dream of Westernization and to realize that the enforced universalization of the Western model, instead of bringing peace and prosperity, will lead to ever bloodier reactions on the part of those whose cultures and ways of life are being destroyed by this process. It is also high time to question the belief in the unique superiority of liberal democracy. Such a belief is at the core of the liberal negation of the political and it constitutes a serious obstacle to the recognition that the world, as Schmitt observed, is not a 'universe' but a 'pluriverse'.

There is another aspect which reveals the anti-political nature of Habermas's approach. His discourse-theoretical understanding of democracy requires ascribing an epistemic function to democratic will-formation and, as he admits himself, 'the democratic procedure no longer draws its legitimizing force only, indeed not even predominantly, from political participation and the expression of political will, but rather from the general accessibility of a deliberative process whose structure grounds an expectation of rationally acceptable results'.[17] What are those 'rationally acceptable results'? Who will decide on the limits to be imposed to the expression of political will? What are going to be the grounds for exclusion? On all those questions that liberals try to avoid, Schmitt is right when he says:

> With regard to these decisive political concepts, it depends on who interprets, defines and uses them; who concretely decides what peace is, what disarmament, what intervention, what public order and security are. One of the most important manifestations of humanity's legal and spiritual life is the fact that whoever has true power is able to determine the content of concepts and words. Caesar dominus et supra grammaticam. Caesar is also lord over grammar.[18]

I have taken the example of Habermas to illustrate the liberal rationalist perspective but I should point out that, if the superiority of liberal democracy is a central tenet of the rationalist approach, such a belief is also shared by other liberals of different theoretical orientations. For instance, we find it also in some theorists who argue for a 'pragmatic' approach such as Richard Rorty. Despite being an eloquent critique of Habermas's rationalist brand of universalism, whose search for 'context-independent' arguments to justify the superiority of liberal democracy he rejects, Rorty nevertheless joins forces with Habermas in desiring its implementation worldwide. This is not to deny the significant differences existing between their respective approaches. Rorty distinguishes between 'universal validity' and 'universal reach' and in his view the universality of liberal democracy should be envisaged according to this second mode, since it is a matter not of rationality but of persuasion and economic progress. His disagreement with Habermas, however, only concerns the way of arriving at a universal consensus, not its very possibility, and he never puts into question the superiority of the liberal way of life.[19]

In fact, Rorty's 'postmodern bourgeois liberalism' could serve as another example of the liberal negation of the political in its antagonistic dimension. For Rorty, politics is something to be deliberated about in banal, familiar terms. It is a matter of pragmatic, short-term reforms and compromises and democracy is basically a question of people becoming 'nicer' to each other and behaving in a more tolerant way. What 'we liberals' should do is to encourage tolerance and minimize suffering and to persuade other people of the worth of liberal institutions. Democratic politics consists in letting an increasing number of people count as members of our moral and conversational 'we'. He is convinced that, thanks to economic growth and the right kind of 'sentimental education', a consensus can be built worldwide around liberal democratic institutions.

To be sure, Rorty is not a rationalist and he is happy to go along with those who envisage the subject as a social construction, but he cannot accept that social objectivity is constructed through acts of power. This is why he is unable to acknowledge the hegemonic dimension of discursive practices and the fact that power is at the very core of the constitution of identities. This would of course force him to come to terms with the antagonistic dimension that is foreclosed by his liberal framework. Like Habermas he wants to retain the vision of a consensus that would not imply any form of exclusion and the availability of some form of realization of universality. This is why, no more than the Habermasian discourse-theoretical approach, can Rorty's pragmatism provide an adequate framework for a pluralist democratic politics.

Five

When it comes to envisaging the kind of world order better suited to accommodate the democratic demands of a plurality of different constituencies, we find a similar evasion of the antagonistic dimension of the political. This is indeed one of the main shortcomings of the cosmopolitan approach, which, under different guises, is presented as the solution to our present predicament. A lot is at stake in the current debate about the most desirable type of world order and this is why we need to examine carefully the arguments of those who assert that with the end of the bipolar world the opportunity now exists for the establishment of a cosmopolitan world order. The theorists associated with this trend claim that, with the disappearance of the communist enemy, antagonisms are a thing of the past and that, in times of globalization, the cosmopolitan ideal elaborated by Kant can finally be realized.

Despite recent setbacks which have dampened the post-cold war optimism about the establishment of the 'new world order', cosmopolitan views are still very fashionable and influential. However, I will take issue with them in this chapter, showing how the dream of a cosmopolitan future partakes of the negation of 'the political' which I have brought to the fore when examining the other aspects of the post-political perspective. Against the cosmopolitans I will assert that we

It is not worth spending much time on this uncritical celebration of neo-liberal hegemony. Its ideological bias is evident and it does not leave any space for politics. Everything is subordinated to the economic realm and the sovereignty of the market. The democratic version is more interesting because it does not see globalization as a merely economic, self-regulating process and it attributes a greater role to politics than its neo-liberal counterpart does. Different perspectives exist among its proponents which, as Nadia Urbinati has indicated,[1] can be traced back to the way they envisage the relationship between civil society and politics. She distinguishes for instance between those who, like Richard Falk, privilege civil society as the principal locus of democracy and those who, like David Held and Daniele Archibugi, put the emphasis on the political realm and on the exercise of citizenship which in their view needs to be extended beyond the nation-state in order to become cosmopolitan. Urbinati notes that the civil society approach 'shares a liberal anti-coercive view of politics and interprets democracy more as a civic culture of association, participation and mobilization than as a political process of decision-making'.[2] The political approach, on the contrary, stresses the importance of establishing relations between civil society and the political sphere: 'it acknowledges social movements and non-governmental organizations as fundamental components of global democracy but it also believes that in the absence of institutionalized procedures of decision and control, social movements and NGO's can be both exclusionary and hierarchical'.[3] This is why they insist that a self-governing civil society is not enough and that a legal and institutional framework is needed to secure equality and to prevent social interests from asserting their dominance at the expense of justice.

DEMOCRATIC TRANSNATIONALISM

Let us look first at the civil society approach. In his more recent work, written jointly with Andrew Strauss, Richard Falk has put forward a vision of 'democratic transnationalism', the aim of which is to achieve human security in the international sphere. It is an approach which 'calls for the resolution of political conflict through an open transnational citizen/societal (rather than state or market) centred political process legitimized by fairness, adherence to human rights, the rule of law, and representative community participation'.[4] The core of this democratic transnationalism is to be constituted by a Global Parliamentary Assembly (GPA) providing a global institutional voice for the people of the world.[5] Falk and Strauss present the mission of such an assembly – whose powers should always be exercised according to the Universal Declaration of Human Rights – as contributing to the democratization of global policy, not only in its formulation but also in its implementation. We need, they say, an international framework to accommodate the current internationalization of civic politics, and this GPA could provide the beginnings of a democratic form of accountability for the international system. The authors also believe that such a GPA could play a role in encouraging compliance with human rights norms. Indeed, given the lack of reliable mechanisms to implement many of the laws accepted by the international system, the GPA could put moral pressure on states by exposing their human rights failures.

Since 11 September 2001, Falk and Strauss have reiterated their proposal, insisting that the creation of a GPA represents an alternative to the statist response centred on national security. As we saw in the last chapter, they see the growth of terrorism as the dark side of the transnationalization of politics.

Its grievances, membership and targets are all transnational, and state-centric structures are therefore inadequate to address the forms of frustration which foster its growing appeal. The solution lies, in their view, in the creation of an institutional framework capable of democratically accommodating the growing internationalization of politics so that 'Individuals and groups could channel their frustrations into efforts to attempt to participate in and influence parliamentary decision-making as they have become accustomed to doing in the more democratic societies of the world'.[6]

I agree that, instead of being perceived as the expression of a few evil and pathological individuals, terrorism has to be situated into a wider geopolitical context, but I find their solution thoroughly inadequate. The main shortcoming of democratic transnationalism is that, like traditional liberalism, it sees the state as the main problem and believes that the solution lies in civil society. Falk and Strauss assert that

> We believe that the underlying preconditions for a GPA are being created by the way that civic politics is increasingly challenging the autonomy of the state-centric international system. In one of the most significant, if still under-recognized, developments of the last several years, both civic voluntary organizations and business and financial elites are engaged in creating parallel structures that complement and erode the traditionally exclusive role of states as the only legitimate actors in the global political system. Individuals and groups, and their numerous transnational associations, rising up from and challenging the confines of territorial states, are promoting 'globalization-from-below', and have begun to coalesce into what is now recognized as being a rudimentary 'global civil society'. Business and financial

elites, on their side, acting largely to facilitate economic globalization, have launched a variety of mechanisms to promote their own preferred global policy initiatives, a process that can be described as 'globalization-from-above'.[7]

According to our authors, citizens, groups and business and financial elites are beginning to recognize that they have a common interest in mounting a challenge to states which should cease to act as their representatives in the international arena. They are convinced that many of the leading figures in world business, like those who meet at the economic summit every January in Davos, have an enlightened sense of their long-term interests and are very sympathetic to the idea of democratizing the international system. The organized networks of global civil society and business should therefore be able to impose their democratizing projects on the reluctant governments. The objective is the unification of globalization-from-below and globalization-from-above in order to establish a global institutional democratic structure enabling the people of the world to bypass the states and have a meaningful voice in global governance, thereby creating a peaceful global order. Like the theorists of 'reflexive modernity', they envisage the progress of democracy on the model of a dialogue among particular interests, a dialogue through which an 'international community' based on consensus could be established.

It is not surprising that similar ideas about the possible alliance between the forces of civil society and transnational corporations are found in the work of Ulrich Beck, whose thesis about the end of the adversarial form of politics I discussed in Chapter 3. In an article where he endorses the cosmopolitan perspective, this is how he envisages the future:

> In the short term, protectionist forces may triumph, a
> heterogeneous mix of nationalists, anticapitalists,
> environmentalists, defenders of national democracy as well
> as xenophobic groupings and religious fundamentalists. In
> the long term, however, an even more paradoxical coalition
> between the supposed 'losers' from globalizations (trade
> unions, environmentalists, democrats) and the 'winners' (big
> business, financial markets, world trade organizations, the
> World Bank) may indeed lead to a renewal of the political –
> provided that both sides recognize that their specific interests
> are best served by cosmopolitan rules.[8]

Celebrating the emergence of 'cosmopolitan corporations'
and 'cosmopolitan capitalism', Beck criticizes the national
fixation with politics and declares that state-centred concepts
of power and politics are 'zombie categories'. The mission of
a cosmopolitan social science is to debunk this old-fashioned
model and to promote the idea of 'deterritorialized' and
'denationalized' states. The future lies in the 'cosmopolitan
state' founded on the principle of lack of national differentiation. Such a state, endowed with 'cosmopolitan sovereignty',
would guarantee genuine diversity and establish fundamental
human rights. Beck gives Europe as example of this cosmopolitan state, adding that there is no reason for this model not
to be extended to the rest of the world. It is, in his view, the
very development of capitalism which pushes toward a global
cosmopolitan transformation. Although put in the interroga-
tive mode, he even suggests 'Could capitalism become a factor
in the cosmopolitan revival of democracy?'[9] No need to be
very perspicacious to guess what his answer is!

COSMOPOLITICAL DEMOCRACY

The political version of cosmopolitanism stresses that democracy is exercised not only in civil society but also in the political arena. It is in order to highlight this specificity that Daniele Archibugi has recently proposed to call 'cosmopolitical' instead of 'cosmopolitan' the approach which, jointly with David Held, he has been elaborating since the book they edited together in 1995, *Cosmopolitan Democracy: An Agenda for a New World Order*. Archibugi defines their project in the following way:

> Cosmopolitical democracy is based on the assumption that important objectives – control of the use of force, respect for human rights, self-determination – will be obtained only through the extension and development of democracy. It differs from the general approach to cosmopolitanism in that it does not merely call for global responsibility but actually attempts to apply the principles of democracy internationally. For such problems as the protection of the environment, the regulation of migration and the use of natural resources to be subjected to necessary democratic control, democracy must trascend the border of single states and assert itself on global level.[10]

According to the cosmopolitical perspective, there is no reason why, now that the democratic form of government is recognized worldwide as the only legitimate one, the principles and rules of democracy should stop at the borders of a political community. This calls for the creation of new global institutions. In their view, it would be a mistake to believe that a set of democratic states automatically entails a democratic globe and global democracy cannot be envisaged as the direct result of democracy within states. It requires the creation of special procedures and institutions that would add another level of political representation to the existing one. Moreover, it is not a matter of simply transposing the democratic model as conceived at state level on to a world scale, and many aspects of this model need to be reformulated in order to be applied globally. Archibugi does not advocate the end of nation-states and he asserts that a global level of representation could coexist with the already constituted states which would keep some of their political and administrative functions. He stresses that 'unlike the many world-federalist projects to which it is indebted, cosmopolitan democracy aims to boost the management of human affairs at a planetary level not so much by replacing existing states as by granting more powers to existing institutions and creating new ones'.[11] The time has come, he claims, to imagine new forms of democracy derived from the universal rights of global citizens, and he suggests that moving from national to global democracy means something akin to the conceptual revolution which in the eighteenth century allowed the passage from direct to representative democracy.

Such a revolution would consist in the creation of international institutions allowing individuals to have an influence on global affairs, independently of the situation in their own countries. The demands of all the individuals, irrespective of their national origin, of their class, gender, etc., should be given a direct form of representation at world level. This might look like an attractive prospect, but how is it to be done? Some information is provided by David Held, who distinguishes between short-term and long-term objectives. To begin with, the following measures should be implemented.[12] The UN Security Council needs to be reformed to become more representative and a second UN chamber created jointly with regional parliaments. Next to that, the influence of international courts should be extended to enforce a cluster of key rights, civil, political, economic and social and a new international Human Rights Court should be established. Finally an effective and accountable international military force would have to be established to intervene against states who are repeatedly violating those rights. In the long term, Held envisages a more radical shift towards global democratic governance with the formation of an authoritative assembly of all democratic states and agencies with the authority to decide on all important global issues dealing with the environment, health, diet, economy, war, etc. According to him, there should be a permanent shift of a growing proportion of the coercive military capacities of the nation-state to global institutions with the aim of transcending the war system as a means of resolving conflict.

Another important aspect of Held's cosmopolitan framework is the entrenchment of democratic rights and obligations in national and international law. Here the aim is 'to create the basis of a common structure of political action as constituting the elements of a democratic public law'.[13] However, to be effective in the context of globalization, such democratic law must be internationalized, it must be transformed into a cosmopolitan democratic law. He argues that the aim of all democrats should be to establish a cosmopolitan community, i.e. a transnational structure of political action, a community of all democratic communities. Discussing the consequences of such a transnational community for the nation-state, he declares that it will 'wither away', not in the sense that it will become redundant but in the sense that

states can no longer be, and can no longer be regarded as,
the sole centres of legitimate power within their own borders,
as is already the case in diverse settings. States need to be
articulated with, and relocated within, an overarching
democratic law. Within this framework, the laws and rules of
the nation-state would be but one focus for legal
development, political reflection and mobilization. For this
framework would respecify and reconstitute the meaning and
limits of sovereign authority. Particular power centers and
authority systems would enjoy legitimacy only to the extent
that they upheld and enacted democratic law.[14]

It is not in my intention to deny the noble intentions of
the diverse advocates of democratic cosmopolitanism.
Unfortunately there are many reasons to be more than sceptical about the democratizing impact of the cosmopolitical
approach. To begin with, as Danilo Zolo has convincingly
argued,[15] given the enormous disparity of power among
its members, it is completely unrealistic to believe in the
possibility of reforming the United Nations in order simultaneously to strengthen them and to make them more democratic. The central proposal of the cosmopolitans is therefore
revealed as impracticable. But one should also be aware of the
consequences arising from the attempt to extend the concept
of rights beyond the nation-state. David Chandler is indeed
right when he points out[16] that, without a mechanism that
would allow for making those new rights accountable to their
subjects, cosmopolitan rights are fictitious. Given that the
global citizen can be represented only through global civil
society which acts outside the representative framework of
liberal democracy, such rights are outside the control of their
subject and they are necessarily dependent on the advocacy of

On the Political

the agency of civil society institutions. The danger of those rights without subjects is that they may be used to undermine existing democratic rights of self-government as when civil society institutions challenge national sovereignty in the name of 'global concern'.

Like Habermas, whose conception of human rights I discussed in Chapter 4, the cosmopolitical approach puts more emphasis on the legitimating function of human rights than on their democratic exercise, and I agree with Chandler that the cosmopolitan construction of the global citizen is another attempt to privilege morality over politics. As he puts it:

> In this respect, cosmopolitan theorists reflect broader political trends towards the privileging of advocacy rights over the representational democracy of the ballot box. Political activity is increasingly undertaken outside the traditional political parties and is becoming a sphere dominated by advocacy groups and single issues campaigns who do not seek to garner votes but to lobby or gain publicity for their claims.[17]

The new rights of cosmopolitan citizens are therefore a chimera: they are moral claims, not democratic rights that could be exercised.

There is an even more serious problem, however, which is that, in exchange for those fictitious new rights, the cosmopolitan approach ends up sacrificing the old rights of sovereignty. By justifying the right for international institutions to undermine sovereignty in order to uphold cosmopolitan law, it denies the democratic rights of self-government for the citizens of many countries. Chandler notes that 'Cosmopolitan regulation is in fact based on the concept of sovereign inequality, that not all states should be equally involved in the establishment and adjudication of international law. Ironically, the new cosmopolitan forms of justice and rights protection involve law-making and law-enforcement, legitimized from an increasingly partial, and explicitly Western perspective.'[18]

Remember for instance how Held presents his cosmopolitan community as a community of 'all democratic states'. Who will decide which states are democratic, and on what criteria? No doubt it is the Western conception of democracy that will be used. It is rather telling that Held does not see that as a problem. When examining how democratic law should be enforced he asserts, 'In the first instance, cosmopolitan democratic law could be promulgated and defended by those democratic states and civil societies that are able to muster the necessary political judgement and to learn how political practices and institutions must change and adapt in the new regional and global circumstances.'[19]

In a recent book,[20] Held has specified further the nature of the cosmopolitan order that he advocates. He stresses that he wants to offer a social democratic alternative to the current type of globalization, whose motor is a US-designed neo-liberal economic project. According to him, what is at stake is the establishment of a new internationalism informed by cosmopolitan values and standards. Cosmopolitanism asserts a set of basic values and standards which no agent should be able to violate, and it requires forms of political regulation and law-making which go beyond the powers and constraints of the nation-states. Such a cosmopolitanism, he says, 'can be taken as the moral and political outlook which builds on the strengths of the liberal multilateral order, particularly its commitment to universal standards, human rights and democratic values, and which seeks to specify general principles on which all could act'.[21] Those principles are the following:

equal worth and dignity; active agency; personal responsibility and accountability; consent; collective decision-making about public matters through voting procedures; inclusiveness and subsidiarity; avoidance of serious harm and sustainability. Taken together they constitute the guiding ethical basis of global social democracy.

Held's project certainly represents a progressive alternative to the current neo-liberal order. However, for all the reasons that we have seen, it is clear that the cosmopolitan framework, even when formulated from a social democratic standpoint, would not increase the possibility of self-government for global citizens. Whatever its guise, the implementation of a cosmopolitan order would in fact result in the imposition of one single model, the liberal democratic one, on to the whole world. In fact it would mean bringing more people directly under the control of the West, with the argument that its model is the better suited to the implementation of human rights and universal values. And, as I have argued, this is bound to arouse strong resistances and to create dangerous antagonisms.

DEMOCRACY AND GLOBAL GOVERNANCE

The post-political character of the cosmopolitan perspective is clearly brought to the fore when we examine one of its central concepts, the concept of 'governance'.[22] Scrutinizing the difference between 'government' and 'governance', Nadia Urbinati specifies that

> Governance entails an explicit reference to 'mechanisms' or 'organized' and 'coordinated activities' appropriate to the solution of some specific problems. Unlike government, governance refers to 'policies' rather than 'politics' because it is not a binding decision-making structure. Its recipients are

> not 'the people' as a collective political subject, but 'the
> population' that can be affected by global issues such as the
> environment, migration or the use of natural resources.[23]

Speaking of global governance tells us a lot about the type of actor which the cosmopolitans see as being active in their model. The central issue in global governance is the negotiation among a diversity of associations and interest groups with specific expertise, intervening in particular issues and trying to push forward their proposals in a non-adversarial way. This implies a conception of politics as resolution of technical problems, not active engagement of citizens exercising their democratic rights thanks to an 'agonistic' confrontation about conflicting hegemonic projects. To be sure, some of those associations are motivated by ethical concerns and not merely by interest but their approach is not a properly political one. Their aim is to reach a compromise or a rational consensus, not to challenge the prevailing hegemony. Such a perspective, no doubt, chimes with the liberal understanding of politics and its fits perfectly the consensual vocabulary of the third way. But in what sense can this form of global governance still be considered as democratic?

Robert Dahl clearly answers that it cannot and he criticizes the celebration of international organizations by cosmopolitan advocates who see them as a further step in the long march of the democratic idea from the *polis* to the cosmos. For Dahl, this is a view of democracy that leaves aside the fact that all decisions, even those made by democratic governments, are disadvantageous to some people because, if their produce gains, they also have costs. 'If the trade-offs in advantages and disadvantages were identical for everyone, judgments involved in making collective decisions would be roughly equivalent to those involved in making individual decisions: but the trade-offs are not the same for everyone.'[24] Costs and benefits are therefore distributed unevenly and the central question is always: who should decide and on whose criteria? Hence the importance for those decisions to be open to contestation. If this is already difficult at the national level, it becomes almost intractable when one considers the case of a hypothetical international *demos* where great differences exist in the magnitude of the population and the power of the different states.

Dahl argues that, if we accept that democracy is a system of popular control over governmental policies and decisions, one has to conclude that international decision-making cannot be democratic. This does not mean seeing international organizations as undesirable and negating their usefulness. But he claims that there is 'no reason to clothe international organizations in the mantle of democracy simply in order to provide them with greater legitimacy'.[25] He proposes instead to treat them as 'bureaucratic bargaining systems' that might be necessary but whose costs to democracy should be acknowledged and taken into account when decisions are made about ceding them important national powers.

Mary Kaldor is also sceptical about the idea that democratic procedures could be reconstituted at the global level. But, contrary to Dahl, she endorses the cosmopolitan project and she suggests an ingenious solution: to envisage global civil society as a functional equivalent to democracy.[26] According to her, once we acknowledge that the central issue in parliamentary democracy has always been one of deliberation, not representation, the difficulties linked to the establishment of a global representative democracy can be ignored. Participation in a global civil society could replace representation by providing a place for deliberation about the range of issues affecting people in different aspects of their lives. Even if we leave aside the very problematic notion of 'global civil society', there are serious difficulties with such an idea. For a start, mere deliberation without the moment of decision and the mechanisms to enforce those decisions means very little. If we add to that the privilege that she attributes to advocacy groups, it becomes evident that, in the name of adapting it to the age of globalization, her proposal ends up depriving the notion of democracy of one of its important dimensions. To be sure, Kaldor defends a very activist conception of civil society and she stresses the need for a redistribution of power. Her views are on several points rather radical but she clearly partakes of the consensual approach. According to her, civil society is the locus of a type of governance based on consent, a consent which is generated through politics conceived as 'social bargaining'. She believes in the possibility of 'a genuinely free conversation, a rational critical dialogue', and is convinced that 'through access, openness and debate, policy makers are more likely to act as an Hegelian universal class, in the interests of the human community'.[27]

As should be clear by now, the central problem with the diverse forms of cosmopolitanism is that they all postulate, albeit in different guises, the availability of a form of consensual governance transcending the political, conflict and negativity. The cosmopolitan project is therefore bound to deny the hegemonic dimension of politics. In fact several cosmopolitan theorists explicitly state that their aim is to envisage a politics 'beyond hegemony'. Such an approach overlooks the fact that since power relations are constitutive of the social, every order is by necessity a hegemonic order. To believe in the possibility of a cosmopolitan democracy with

On the Political

cosmopolitan citizens with the same rights and obligations, a constituency that would coincide with 'humanity' is a dangerous illusion. If such a project was ever realized, it could only signify the world hegemony of a dominant power that would have been able to impose its conception of the world on the entire planet and which, identifying its interests with those of humanity, would treat any disagreement as an illegitimate challenge to its 'rational' leadership.

AN ABSOLUTE DEMOCRACY OF THE MULTITUDE?

If the cosmopolitical approach is not able to provide the political perspective required by the age of globalization, what about the vision put forward by Michael Hardt and Antonio Negri in *Empire*,[28] a book that has been hailed as 'The Communist Manifesto for the Twenty-first Century'? Some people seem indeed to believe that this is the answer that the left has been waiting for. However, as I will show in a moment, a close examination reveals an unexpected convergence between *Empire* and liberal cosmopolitanism. In both cases what is missing is the properly political dimension: power can be overcome, the constitutive character of antagonism is denied, and the central question of sovereignty is dismissed. *Empire* in fact is no more than an ultra-left version of the cosmopolitan perspective. Far from empowering us, it contributes to reinforcing the current incapacity to think and act politically.

This is not the place for a discussion of all the aspects of the book. As the various critiques have revealed, behind the wide range of references and topics which have seduced so many readers, its basic theses do not stand scrutiny. Very little indeed has been left standing of the main argument. Not only have the theoretical analyses about the importance of immaterial labour, the role of the nation-state, the homogenizing effects of global capital and the revolutionary nature of the 'multitude' been drastically challenged.[29] In a very spectacular way, the central tenet of the book, the end of imperialism and the emergence of a new form of sovereignty without a centre, has been shattered by the wars waged by the United States after the the the terrorist attacks of 11 September 2001. I find it amazing that even in *Multitude, War and Democracy in the Age of Empire*,[30] which came out in 2004, they do not really put into question their claim that 'there is no center of imperial power.'[31]. To be sure, the first part is dedicated to examining the characteristics of the new wars and they acknowledge the pivotal role of the United States. But they refuse to see it as an imperialist power; it is only a unilateralist version of empire which they insist in presenting as a decentred network power. The only difference is that, while their previous book was very assertive about the actual existence of empire, they now insist that they are only indicating a *tendency* manifest in a number of contemporary processes.

How can we explain the success of such a flawed book? In the post-political period in which we are living, with neo-liberal globalization being perceived as the unique horizon, it is not surprising that *Empire* with its messianic rhetoric has fired the imagination of many people eager to find in the 'multitude' a new revolutionary subject. Its visionary character brought hope in a time where the success of capitalism seemed so complete that no alternative could be envisaged. The problem of course is that, instead of contributing to working towards an alternative to the current neo-liberal hegemony, *Empire* is in fact likely to produce the opposite effect. If, as I have been arguing, what is needed today is an adequate understanding of the nature of the political which will permit grasping the conditions for an effective hegemonic challenge to the neo-liberal order, we certainly do not find in this book the theoretical tools for such an enterprise. What we find is another version of the post-political perspective which defines the common sense in our post-democracies. To be sure, in this case it is a 'radical' version, formulated in a sophisticated philosophical vocabulary: hence its appeal to those who pretend that the time has come to relinquish 'old-fashioned' categories and 'rethink' the political.

However, despite the Deleuzian terminology and the revolutionary rhetoric, there are many uncanny similarities between Hardt's and Negri's views and the third way theorists and cosmopolitan liberals advocating the need to 'rethink politics'. Take for instance the question of globalization. All those theorists see globalization as a progressive step whose homogenizing consequences are creating the conditions for a more democratic world. The demise of the sovereignty of the nation-states is perceived as a new stage in the emancipation from the constraints of the state. A global polity is being established which will permit a new form of global governance. Leaving aside the vacuous rhetoric of the multitude, one can perfectly well see Empire as another version of the cosmopolitan view. Indeed, Hardt's and Negri's insistence on the 'smooth' character of empire and the creation by global capitalism of a unified world without any 'outside' fits remarkably well with the cosmopolitan vision. Similarly, their underestimating of the crucial role played by the United States in the imposition of a neo-liberal model of globalization worldwide chimes with the optimistic view held by the advocates of global civil society.

As far as 'sovereignty' is concerned, there is not so much difference either between those who celebrate the perspective of a universal order organized around a 'cosmopolitan sovereignty' and the radical 'anti-sovereignty' stand taken in *Empire*. In both cases there is a clear desire to do away with the modern concept of sovereignty in the name of a supposedly more democratic form of governance. Cosmopolitan theorists would certainly not disagree with Hardt's and Negri's declaration that 'We need to develop a political theory without sovereignty'.[32]

With respect to the diverse forms of social democratic politics, there is a striking convergence between the theses put forward in *Empire* and those of Beck and Giddens. As Michael Rustin observed, 'They share with the post-socialists of the "Third Way" the view that we now have to accept a new individualized, globalized, networked society as the only possible basis for future action, though the action they envisage is apocalyptic where the reformist post-socialists seek only to mitigate and regulate somewhat the turbulences of global capitalism, to which they envisage no conceivable alternative'.[33] Hence their negative attitude towards the struggles to defend the national welfare states, which in the case of Hardt and Negri also includes a dismissal of the importance of the European Union.

But it is when it comes to envisaging the way an alternative to empire can be brought about that the anti-political character of the book clearly comes to the fore, and that its influence can have the more damaging consequences. Indeed, for a book which presents itself as offering a new vision of radical politics, *Empire* is seriously lacking in political strategy. How can one envisage the political challenge of empire by the multitude? The multitude, they say, is a logical hypothesis which proceeds from their analysis of the economic, political and cultural structures of empire. It is a counter-empire

success of *Empire* is also certainly due to the fact that it seemed to provide a political language for the growing anti-globalization movement. Although various sectors of the traditional ultra-left have tried to reclaim those struggles, presenting them as anti-capitalist working-class struggles, a different theorization is clearly needed. This is where the Deleuzian vocabulary mobilized by Hardt and Negri can be seductive. It allows for the multiplicity of the resistances expressed by this global movement to resonate with the notions elaborated by Deleuze and Guattari in *Anti-Oedipus* and *A Thousand Plateaus*. Nevertheless, I am convinced that it would be a serious mistake for the anti-globalization movement to adopt the perspective put forward in *Empire*. One of the main challenges this 'movement of movements' faces is how to transform itself into a *political* movement putting forward concrete alternative proposals. True, the first steps have already been taken with the organization of the World Social Forums as well as different regional ones. But many important issues concerning the future are still undecided and they will determine its shape and possibilities of success in the years to come.

A fundamental issue concerns the type of relation to be established between the different components of the movement. As is often pointed out, its is a very heterogeneous movement and, while diversity can no doubt be a source of strength, it can also pose serious problems. Hardt and Negri take it for granted that the immanent powers of the multitude will defeat the constituted power of empire. Not surprisingly they never pose the question of political articulation among the different struggles; indeed this is the very question which is foreclosed by their perspective. According to them, the fact that all those struggles do not communicate, far from being a problem, turns out to be a virtue since 'precisely because all these struggles are incommunicable and thus blocked from traveling horizontally in the form of a cycle, they are forced instead to leap vertically and touch immediately on the global level'.[35] In consequence, despite its local origin, each struggle directly attacks the virtual centre of empire. Hardt and Negri exhort us to relinquish the model of horizontal articulation of struggles which is no longer adequate and blinds us to the new radical potential. No need to worry any more about how to articulate a diversity of movements with different interests and whose demands might be in conflict. In that way, the central question of democratic politics, the question which the anti-globalization movement needs urgently to address – how to organize across differences so as to create a chain of equivalence among democratic struggles – this question is simply vaporized.

Another serious problem lies in the very negative way in which local and national struggles are envisaged in *Empire*. This is of course in tune with Hardt's and Negri's vilification of sovereignty and their celebration of globalization, presented as establishing a 'smooth' space where national sovereignties and obstacles to the free movement of the multitude are being swept away. According to them, the process of 'deterritorialization' and the concomitant weakening of nation-states characteristic of empire represents a step forward in the liberation of the multitude and they reject any form of politics nationally or regionally based. In their view, the valorization of the local is regressive and fascistic and they declare that 'The multitude's resistance to bondage – the struggles against the slavery of belonging to a nation, an identity, and a people, and thus the desertion from sovereignty and the limits it places on subjectivity is, entirely positive'.[36]

Were the anti-globalization movement to adopt such a

perspective, it would, no doubt, condemn itself to political irrelevance. Indeed, its future and impact lie in its capacity to organize at a multiplicity of different levels, local, national, regional as well as global. Despite the claims made in Empire, nation-states are still important players and, even if it is true that multinational companies operate according to strategies largely independent from the states, they cannot dispense with the power of the states. As Doreen Massey stresses,[37] the globalized space is 'striated', with a diversity of sites where relations of power are articulated in specific local, regional and national configurations. The multiplicity of nodal points calls for a variety of strategies, and the struggle cannot simply be envisaged at the global level. Regional and local forums such as those which have been organized in Europe (Florence in 2002, Paris in 2003, London in 2004) and in many cities of the world are the places where a variety of resistances can become interconnected and where the 'war of position' – to borrow a term from Gramsci – can be launched. Local and national allegiances can also provide important sites of resistance and to dismiss them, refusing to mobilize their affective dimension around democratic objectives, is to leave this potential available for articulation by right-wing demagogues. For the anti-globalization movement to follow Hardt's and Negri's advice and to see those allegiances as reactionary would be a serious mistake.

Against the fallacious picture of a global multitude facing a unified empire, a confrontation which will inevitably result in the victory of the multitude and 'the invention of a new democracy, an absolute democracy, unbounded, immeasurable,'[38] the question that needs to be addressed concerns the political forms of organizations of the resistances, and this requires acknowledging the divisions existing within both sides.

Neither the conflicts among the 'desiring machines' of the multitude, nor the divergence of interests within the capitalist camp should be overlooked. Hardt's and Negri's vision of a globalized smooth space, like the cosmopolitan perspective, fails to appreciate the pluralistic nature of the world, the fact that it is a 'pluriverse' not a 'universe'. Their idea of an 'absolute democracy', a state of radical immanence beyond sovereignty, where a new form of self-organization of the multitude would replace a power-structured order, is the postmodern form of longing for a reconciled world – a world where desire would have triumphed against order, where the immanent constituent power of the multitude would have defeated the transcendent constituted power of the state, and where the political would have been eliminated. Such a longing, whatever its version – liberal or ultra-left – prevents us from grasping what is the real challenge facing democratic politics at both the domestic and the international level: not how to overcome the we/they relation but how to envisage forms of construction of we/they compatible with a pluralistic order.

TOWARDS A MULTIPOLAR WORLD ORDER

As I have argued in Chapter 4, it is the fact that we are now living in a unipolar world where there are no legitimate channels for opposing the hegemony of the United States which is at the origin of the explosion of new antagonisms which, if we are unable to grasp their nature, might indeed lead to the announced 'clash of civilizations'. The way to avoid such a prospect is to take pluralism seriously instead of trying to impose one single model on the whole world, even if it is a well meaning cosmopolitan one. It is therefore urgent to relinquish the illusion of a unified world and to work towards the establishment of a multipolar world. We hear a lot today about the necessity of an effective 'multilateralism'. But multilateralism in an unipolar world will always be an illusion. As long as a single hegemonic power exists, it will always be the one that decides if it will take into consideration the opinion of other nations or act alone. A real multilateralism requires the existence of a plurality of centres of decision and some sort of equilibrium – even if it is only a relative one – among various power.

As I have suggested in Chapter 4, we can find important insights in Schmitt's writings of the 1950s and early 1960s where he speculated about the possibility of a new Nomos of the Earth that could replace the Jus Publicum Europeaum. In an article from 1952[39] where he examined how the dualism created by the cold war and the polarization between capitalism and communism could evolve, he imagined several possible scenarios. He was sceptical about the idea that such a dualism was only the prelude to a final unification of the world, resulting from the total victory of one of the antagonists which would then be able to impose its system and its ideology worldwide. The end of bipolarity was more likely to lead to new equilibrium guaranteed by the Unites States and under its hegemony. Schmitt also envisaged the possibility of a third form of evolution consisting in the opening of a dynamics of pluralization, the outcome of which could be the establishment of a new global order based on the existence of several autonomous regional blocs. This would provide the conditions for an equilibrium of forces among various large areas, instituting among them a new system of international law. Such an equilibrium would present similarities with the old Jus Publicum Europaeum except that in this case it would be truly global and not only Euro-centric. It was his favoured solution because he believed that, by establishing a 'true pluralism', such a multipolar world order would provide the institutions necessary to manage conflicts and avoid the negative consequences resulting from the pseudo-universalism arising from the generalization of one single system. He was aware, though, that such a pseudo-universalism was a much more likely outcome than the pluralism he advocated. And unfortunately his fears have been confirmed since the collapse of communism.

Schmitt's reflections were of course motivated by concerns very different from mine, but I think that his vision is particularly relevant for our current conjuncture. The left should acknowlege the pluralist character of the world and adopt the multipolar perspective. This, as Massimo Cacciari has argued,[40] means working towards the establishment of an international system of law based on the idea of regional poles and cultural identities federated among themselves in the recognition of their full autonomy. Cacciari acknowledges the pluralist character of the world and, examining the question of the relation with the Islamic world, he warns against the belief that the modernization of Islam should take place through Westernization. Trying to impose our model would, he says, multiply local conflicts of resistance which foment global terrorism. He suggests a model of globalization constructed around a certain number of great spaces and genuine cultural poles and insists that the new order of the world needs to be a multipolar one.

Clearly, given the unquestionable supremacy of the United States, many people will claim that the project of a multipolar world is completely unrealistic. But it is certainly no more unrealistic than the cosmopolitan vision. In fact, the emergence of China as a superpower testifies that such a dynamics of pluralization, far from being unrealistic, is already at work. And this is not the only sign that regional blocs are being formed, the aim of which is to gain some autonomy and power of negotiation. This is for instance clearly the direction that several countries in Latin America are taking under the leadership of Brazil and Argentina in their attempt to strengthen the Mercosur (a shared economic structure in South America); a similar dynamics is at work in the coming together of several East Asian countries in the ASEAN, and the attraction of such a model is likely to grow.

I do not want to minimize the obstacles that need to be overcome, but, at least in the case of the creation of a multipolar order, those obstacles are only of an empirical nature, while the cosmopolitan project is also based on flawed theoretical premises. Its dream of a world order which would not be structured around power relations is based on a refusal to come to terms with the hegemonic nature of every order. Once it is acknowledged that there is no 'beyond hegemony', the only conceivable strategy for overcoming world dependence on a single power is to find ways to 'pluralize' hegemony. And this can be done only through the recognition of a multiplicity of regional powers. It is only in this context that no agent in the international order will be able, because of its power, to regard itself above the law and to arrogate to itself the role of the sovereign. Moreover, as Danilo Zolo has pointed out, 'a multipolar equilibrium is the necessary condition for international law to exercise even that minimal function, which is the containment of the most destructive consequences of modern warfare'.[41]

We are today facing decisive years. After the euphoria of the 1990s where the final victory of liberal democracy and the coming of a 'new world order' were hailed from so many quarters, new antagonims have emerged which represent challenges that decades of neo-liberal hegemony have made us unable to confront. In this book I have examined some of those challenges and I have argued that understanding their nature requires coming to terms with the ineradicable dimension of antagonism which exists in human societies, what I have proposed to call 'the political'.

As far as domestic politics is concerned, I have shown how the belief in the end of an adversarial form of politics and the overcoming of the left/right divide, instead of facilitating the establishment of a pacified society, has created the terrain for the rise of right-wing populist movements. By suggesting that the solution lies in fostering the agonistic character of politics through the revitalization of the left/right distinction, I do not call for a mere return to their traditional content, as if the meaning of those terms had been fixed once and for all. What is at stake in the left/right opposition is not a particular content – although as Norberto Bobbio pointed out it certainly refers to opposing attitudes with respect to social redistribution[1] – but the recognition of social division and the legitimation of conflict. It brings to the fore the existence in a democratic society of a plurality of interests and demands which, although they conflict and can never be finally reconcilied, should nevertheless be considered as legitimate. The very content of left and right will vary, but the dividing line should remain because its disappearance would indicate that social division is denied and that an ensemble of voices has been silenced. This is why democratic politics is by nature necessarily adversarial. As Niklas Luhmann has stressed, modern democracy calls for a 'splitting of the summit', a clear divide between the government and the opposition, and this supposes that clearly differentiated policies are on offer, giving the possibility for citizens to decide between different ways of organizing society.[2] When social division cannot be expressed because of the left/right divide, passions cannot be mobilized towards democratic objectives and antagonisms take forms which can endanger democratic institutions.

THE LIMITS OF PLURALISM

To avoid any confusion, I should specify that, contrary to some postmodern thinkers who envisage a pluralism without any frontiers, I do not believe that a democratic pluralist politics should consider as legitimate all the demands formulated in a given society. The pluralism that I advocate requires discriminating between demands which are to be accepted as part of the agonistic debate and those which are to be excluded. A democratic society cannot treat those who put its basic institutions into question as legitimate adversaries. The agonistic approach does not pretend to encompass all differences and to overcome all forms of exclusions. But exclusions are envisaged in political and not in moral terms. Some demands are excluded, not because they are declared to be

On the Political

'evil', but because they challenge the institutions constitutive of the democratic political association. To be sure, the very nature of those institutions is also part of the agonistic debate, but, for such a debate to take place, the existence of a shared symbolic space is necessary. This is what I meant when I argued in Chapter 2 that democracy requires a 'conflictual consensus': consensus on the ethico-political values of liberty and equality for all, dissent about their interpretation. A line should therefore be drawn between those who reject those values outright and those who, while accepting them, fight for conflicting interpretations.

My position can here appear similar to that of a liberal theorist like John Rawls, whose distinction between 'simple' and 'reasonable' pluralism is also an attempt to draw a line between legitimate and illegitimate demands. However it differs significantly from Rawls's: he pretends that such a discrimination is grounded in rationality and morality, while I claim that the drawing of the frontier between the legitimate and the illegitimate is always a political decision, and that it should therefore always remain open to contestation.[3] Taking my bearings from Wittgenstein, I assert that our allegiance to democratic values and institutions is not based on their superior rationality and that liberal democratic principles can be defended only as being constitutive of our form of life. Contrary to Rawls and Habermas, I do not attempt to present liberal democracy as the model which would be chosen by every rational individual in idealized conditions. This is why I envisage the normative dimension inscribed in political institutions as being of an 'ethico-political' nature, to indicate that it always refers to specific practices, depending on particular contexts, and that it is not the expression of a universal morality. Indeed, since Kant morality is often presented as a realm of universal commands where there is no place for 'rational disagreement'. This is, in my view, incompatible with recognizing the deeply pluralistic character of the world and the irreducible conflict of values.

It is clear that my position on the limits of pluralism has implications for the current debate about multiculturalism and it is worth spelling out some of them. First, we need to distinguish among the different demands collected under the multiculturalist label between those which concern the recognition of strictly cultural mores and customs and those with a directly political nature. I am perfectly aware that this is not an easy thing to do and that there will never be a definitive, clear-cut and satisfactory solution. But one can establish a rough distinction between a set of demands whose satisfaction can be granted without jeopardizing the basic liberal democratic framework and those which would lead to its destruction. This would be the case for instance with demands whose satisfaction would require the implementation of different legal systems according to the ethnic origin or religious beliefs of groups. There are no doubt certain special cases, like that of indigenous people, where exceptions can be made.[4] But legal pluralism cannot become the norm without endangering the permanence of the democratic political association. A democratic society requires the allegiance of its citizens to a set of shared ethico-political principles, usually spelled out in a constitution and embodied in a legal framework, and it cannot allow the coexistence of conflicting principles of legitimacy in its midst. To believe that, in the name of pluralism, some category of immigrants should be granted an exception is, I submit, a mistake which indicates a lack of understanding of the role of the political in the symbolic ordering of social relations. Some forms of legal pluralism have no doubt existed, as for instance in the Ottoman Empire with the 'millet system' (which recognized Muslims, Christians and Jews communities as self-governing units able to impose restrictive religions laws on their own members), but such a system is incompatible with the exercise of democratic citizenship which postulates equality for all the citizens.

A PLURALISM OF MODERNITIES

When we move from domestic to international politics, we encounter a very different type of pluralism which it is necessary to distinguish from the liberal one. The first type of pluralism is characteristic of liberal democracy and it is linked to the end of a substantive conception of the good life and the assertion of individual liberty. This pluralism is embedded in the institutions of liberal democracy, it is part of its ethico-political principles and it has to be accepted by its citizens. But there is also another type of pluralism, a pluralism which undermines the claim of liberal democracy to provide the universal model that all societies should adopt because of its superior rationality. Such a pluralism is the one which is at stake in the multipolar project.

Contrary to what liberal universalists would want us to believe, the Western model of modernity, characterized by the development of an instrumental type of rationality and an atomistic individualism, is not the only adequate way of relating to the world and to others. It might have gained hegemony in the West, but, as many critics have pointed out, even in the West this is far from being the only form of sociality. It is in this vein that intellectual historians have begun criticizing the monolithic idea of the Enlightenment and have revealed the presence of a multiplicity of diverse enlightenments often in rivalry amongst themselves and which have been displaced by the rise of capitalist modernity.

Examining the diverse enlightenments which are now recognized as constitutive of European history – civil, meta-physical, neo-Roman, popular sovereignty and civic – James Tully argues that the question 'What is Enlightenment?', which was formulated within the Kantian tradition as a transcendental question with a definitive transcendental-legislative answer, should be de-transcendentalized and respecified as a historical question 'with diverse small (e) enlightenment answers, each relative to a form of self-proclaimed enlightened subjectivity acquired through the exercise of a particular ethos and its cognate political practices'.[5] However, it is not enough to limit the enquiry to Europe because, once the historical character of the question is recognized, we have to admit that, no more than a definitive transcendental answer, can it receive a definitive historical one. Therefore, as Tully suggests 'the problematization defined by "What is Enlightenment?" should no longer be confined to endless discussions of the rival solutions within Europe and against the background of the European transition to a modern system of sovereign states and its successive modifications'.[6]

I think that Tully's reflections about the possibility of non-Western enlightenments are crucial for the formulation of the multipolar approach. Indeed such an approach requires us to accept that there are other forms of modernity than the one which the West is trying to impose worldwide, irrespective of the respect of other histories and traditions. To defend a model of society different from the Western one should not be seen as an expression of backwardness and proof that one remains in a 'premodern' stage. It is high human rights that would reconceive them as 'multicultural', allowing for different formulations according to different cultures.

Sousa Santos follows the approach of Raimundo Panikkar, who argues that, in order to understand the meaning of human rights, it is necessary to scrutinize the function they play in our culture. This will allow us later to ascertain whether this function is not fulfilled in different ways in other cultures.[8] In Western culture human rights are presented as providing the basic criteria for the recognition of human dignity and as being the necessary condition for political order. The question we need to ask is whether other cultures do not give different answers to the same question; in other words, we should look for functional equivalents of human rights. If we accept that what is at stake in human rights is the dignity of the person, it is clear that this question can be answered in a diversity of ways. What Western culture calls 'human rights' is a culturally specific form of answering this question, an individualistic way specific to liberal culture and which cannot claim to be the only legitimate one.

This seems to me a promising perspective and, like Panikkar and Sousa Santos, I insist on the necessiaty of pluralizing the notion of human rights, so as to prevent them becoming an instrument in the imposition of Western hegemony. To acknowledge a plurality of formulations of the idea of human rights is to bring to the fore their political character. The debate about human rights cannot be envisaged as taking place in a neutral terrain where the imperatives of morality and rationality – as defined by the West – would represent the only legitimate criteria. It is a terrain shaped by power relations where a hegemonic struggle takes place, hence the importance of making room for a plurality of legitimate understandings.

I would like to conclude these reflections about the political by asking: what should be the place of Europe in a multipolar world? Is a truly political Europe possible, a Europe which would also be a real power? Is it even desirable? Clearly, this is a strongly contested issue among both the left and the right. Let us examine the reasons why many people on the left do not see this eventuality in a positive way.[9] Some of them identify Europe with the Western capitalist hegemonic project and argue that a political Europe cannot be more than an internal struggle inside the West between two powers fighting for hegemony. The only difference would be that Europe, instead of following the United States, would become its rival. Even if I believed that the end of the unipolar world would be a positive development, this is of course not the kind of Europe that I advocate. The establishment of a pluralistic world order requires discarding the idea that there is only one possible form of globalization, the prevalent neo-liberal one, not merely having Europe competing for its leadership with the United States. For Europe to assert its identity, it is the very idea of the 'West' that must be questioned, so as to open a dynamics of pluralization which could create the basis for resisting neo-liberal hegemony.

Others on the left are suspicious of European integration because they believe that the nation-state is the necessary space for the exercise of democratic citizenship which is put in jeopardy by European institutions. They see the European project as the Trojan horse of neo-liberalism and as endangering the conquests realized by social democratic parties. I do not deny that there is some ground for their distrust of current European policies, but their mistake is to think that they could resist neo-liberal globalization better at the national level. It is only at the European level that one can start envisaging a possible alternative to neo-liberalism. The fact that, unfortunately, this is not the direction that the European Union has taken, far from making people withdraw from European politics, should convince them of the importance of pursuing their struggle at the European level so as to influence the future shape of Europe.

The internationalists, as we have seen, oppose the idea of a political Europe because they are critical of all types of frontiers and regional forms of belonging. They celebrate the 'deterritorialization' created by globalization which, in their view, establishes the conditions for a truly global world without borders, where the 'nomadic multitude' will be able to circulate freely according to its desire. They claim that the construction of a political Europe would reinforce the tendency to establish a 'fortress Europe' and increase the existing discriminations. Such a possibility should not be dismissed, and in a Europe that defines only itself as competitor to the United States, this would be likely to take place. But the situation would be different in the context of a multipolar world in which big regional units would coexist and where the neo-liberal model of globalization would not be the only one.

While there is a general agreement among those on the left who advocate the idea of a political Europe, that it should promote a different civilizational model and not merely compete with American hegemony, it is also true that not all of them accept the multipolar vision. For instance some liberal universalists, who consider that the Western model of liberal democracy should be adopted worldwide, also advocate a political Europe, which they conceive as showing the way that all other societies should follow. What they defend is in fact a cosmopolitan project since they assert that Europe represents the vanguard in the movement toward the establishment of a universal order based on the worldwide implementation of law and human rights. This is for instance the way in which Habermas conceives the European project.[10] His call to the Europeans in 2003 after the invasion of Iraq to unite and oppose the violations of international law and human rights by the Bush government was certainly welcome. Yet, while agreeing with him about the need to create a strong Europe, I do not follow him in envisaging this move as a first step towards the creation of a cosmopolitan order because I do not accept the universalist premises on which such a vision is based.

In my view a truly *political* Europe can exist only in relation to other political entities, as a part of a multipolar world. If Europe can play a crucial role in the creation of a new world order, it is not through the promotion of a cosmopolitan law that all 'reasonable' humanity should obey but by contributing to the establishment of an equilibrium among regional poles whose specific concerns and traditions will be seen as valuable, and where different vernacular models of democracy will be accepted. This is not to deny that we need a set of institutions to regulate international relations, but those institutions, instead of being organized around a unified power structure, should permit a significant degree of pluralism; *pace* the cosmopolitans, the aim cannot be the universalization of the Western liberal democratic model. The attempt to impose this model, deemed to be the only legitimate one, on recalcitrant societies leads to presenting those who do not accept it as 'enemies' of civilization, thereby creating the conditions of an antagonistic struggle. To be sure there will still be conflicts in a multipolar world but those conflicts are less likely to take an antagonistic form than in a unipolar world.

Notes

TWO   POLITICS AND THE POLITICAL

1 Ernesto Laclau and Chantal Mouffe, *Hegemony and Socialist Strategy: Towards a Radical Democratic Politics*, London, Verso, 1985; Chantal Mouffe, *The Return of the Political*, London, Verso, 1993; Chantal Mouffe, *The Democratic Paradox*, London, Verso, 2000.

2 Carl Schmitt, *The Concept of the Political*, New Brunswick, Rutgers University Press, 1976, p. 70.

3 Ibid., p. 35.

4 Ibid., p. 70.

5 Ibid., p. 37.

6 Jürgen Habermas, 'Reply to Symposium Participants', *Cardozo Law Review*, Vol. 17, 4–5, March 1996, p. 1943.

7 Henry Staten, *Wittgenstein and Derrida*, Oxford, Basil Blackwell, 1985.

8 Ernesto Laclau, *Emancipation(s)*, London, Verso, p. 90.

9 This idea of 'agonism' is developed in my book *The Democratic Paradox*, chapter 4. To be sure, I am not the only one to use that term and they are currently a variety of 'agonistic' theorists. However they generally envisage the political as a space of freedom and deliberation, while for me it is a space of conflict and antagonism. This is what differentiates my agonistic perspective from the one defended by William Connolly, Bonnig Honig or James Tully.

10 Elias Canetti, *Crowds and Power*, London, Penguin, 1960, p. 220.

11 Ibid., p. 222.

12 Ibid., p. 221.

13 Sigmund Freud, *Civilization and Its Discontents*, The Standard Edition, Vol. XXI, London, Vintage, 2001, p. 111.

14 Sigmund Freud, *Group Psychology and the Analysis of the Ego*, The Standard Edition, Vol. XVIII (London, Vintage, 2001), p. 92.

15 Sigmund Freud, *Civilization and Its Discontents*, The Standard Edition, vol. XXI (London, Vintage, 2001), p. 114.

16 Ibid., p. 119.

17 Yannis Stavrakakis, 'Passions of Identification: Discourse, Enjoyment and European Identity', in D. Howarth and J. Torfing (eds), *Discourse Theory and European Politics* (London, Palgrave, forthcoming), p. 4 (manuscript).

18 Slavoj Žižek, *Tarring with the Negative*, Durham, Duke University Press, 1993, p. 201.

19 Ibid., p. 202.

20 Jacques Rancière, *Disagreement*, Minneapolis, University of Minnesota Press, 1991, p. 102 (translation modified).

21 See for instance his critiques in Slavoj Žižek and Glyn Daly, *Conversations with Žižek*, Cambridge, Polity, 2004.

THREE   BEYOND THE ADVERSARIAL MODEL?

1 Ulrich Beck, *The Reinvention of Politics: Rethinking Modernity in the Global Social Order*, Cambridge, Polity Press, 1997, p. 38.

2 Ulrich Beck, 'The Reinvention of Politics: Towards a Theory of Reflexive Modernization', in U. Beck, A. Giddens and S. Lash, *Reflexive Modernization*, Cambridge, Polity Press, 1994, p. 5.

3 Ibid., p. 42.

4 Ibid., p. 18.

5 Ibid., p. 22.

6 Ibid., p. 23.

7 Beck, *The Reinvention of Politics*, pp. 168–9.

8 Anthony Giddens, *Beyond Left and Right*, Cambridge, Polity, 1994, p. 7.

9 Anthony Giddens, *Modernity and Self Identity*, Cambridge, Polity, 1991, p. 214.

10 Giddens, *Beyond Left and Right*, p. 92.

11 Anthony Giddens, *The Third Way*, Cambridge, Polity, 1998, p. 36.

12 Giddens, *Beyond Left and Right*, p. 93.

13 Ibid., pp. 117–24.

14 Ibid., p. 119.

15 Ibid., pp. 130–1.

16 Beck, 'The Reinvention of Politics', p. 178.

17 Perry Anderson, 'Power, Politics and the Enlightenment', in David Miliband (ed.), *Reiventing the Left*, Cambridge, Polity Press, 1994, p. 43.

18 Ernesto Laclau and Chantal Mouffe, *Hegemony and Socialist Strategy: Towards a Radical Democratic Politics*, London, Verso, 1985.

19 Giddens, *The Third Way*, p. 27.

20 Ibid., p. 64.

21 Ibid., p. 100.

22 Stuart Hall, 'New Labour's Double-Shuffle', *Soundings*, 24, Autumn 2003.

23 Ibid., p. 18.

24 John Gray, 'Blair's Project in Retrospect', *International Affairs*, Vol. 80, 1, January 2004, 43.

FOUR   CURRENT CHALLENGES TO THE POST-POLITICAL VISION

1 For a detailed analysis of the Austrian case see Chantal Mouffe, 'The End of Politics and the Challenge of Right-Wing Populism', in Francisco Panizza (ed.), *Populism and the Shadow of Democracy*, London, Verso, 2005.

2 A good interpretation of the Vlaams Blok's success is provided by Patrick de Vos in 'The Sacralisation of Consensus and the Rise of Authoritarian Populism: the Case of the Vlaams Blok', *Studies in Social and Political Thought*, 7, September 2002.

3 François Flahaut, *Malice*, London, Verso 2003, p. 117.

4 Carl Schmitt, *The Concept of the Political*, New Brunswick, Rutgers University Press, 1976, p. 54.

5 William Rasch, 'Human Rights as Geopolitics: Carl Schmitt and the Legal Form of American Supremacy', in *Cultural Critique*, 54, Spring 2003, p. 123.

6 Carl Schmitt, *The Nomos of the Earth in the International Law of the Jus Publicum Europaeum*, New York, Telos Press, 2003, p. 321.

7 Carl Schmitt, *Theorie du partisan*, Paris, Calmann-Lévy, 1972, p. 310. German edition: *Theorie des Partisanen*, Berlin, Duncker & Humblot, 1963.

8 Jean-François Kervégan, 'Ami ou ennemi?', in *La Guerre des dieux*, special issue of *Le Nouvel Observateur*, January 2002.

9 Richard Falk and Andrew Strauss, 'The Deeper Challenges of Global Terrorism: a Democritizing Response', in Daniele Archibugi (ed.), *Debating Cosmopolitics*, London, Verso, 2003, p. 206.

10 Jürgen Habermas, *Between Facts and Norms*, Cambridge, MA, MIT Press, 1998, p. 449.

11 Ibid., p. 455.

12 Jürgen Habermas, *The Postnational Constellation*, Cambridge, Polity, 2001, p. 116.

13 Jürgen Habermas, *The Inclusion of the Other*, Cambridge, MA, MIT Press, 1998, p. 192.

14 Habermas, *The Postnational Constellation*, p. 121.

15 Ibid., p. 124.

16 William Rasch, 'Human Rights', p. 142.

17 Habermas, *The Postnational Constellation*, p. 110.

18 Carl Schmitt, 'Völkerrechtliche Formen des modernen Imperialismus', in *Positionen und Begriffe*, Berlin, Duncker & Humbolt, 1988, p. 202.

19 See for instance, Richard Rorty, *Objectivity, Relativism and Truth*, Cambridge, Cambridge University Press, 1991, part III.

FIVE   WHICH WORLD ORDER: COSMOPOLITAN OR MULTIPOLAR?

1 Nadia Urbinati, 'Can Cosmopolitical Democracy Be Democratic?', in Daniele Archibugi (ed.), *Debating Cosmopolitics*, London Verso, 2003, pp. 67–85.

2 Ibid., p. 69.

3 Ibid.

4 Richard Falk and Andrew Strauss, 'The Deeper Challenges of Global Terrorism: a Democratizing Response', in *Debating Cosmopolitics*, p. 203.

5 Richard Falk and Andrew Strauss, 'Towards Global Parliament', *Foreign Affairs*, January–February 2001.

6 Falk and Strauss, 'The Deeper Challenges of Global Terrorism', p. 205.

7 Ibid., p. 209.

8 Ulrich Beck, 'Redefining Power in the Global Age: Eight Theses', *Dissent*, Fall 2001, p. 89.

9 Ibid.

10 Daniele Archibugi, 'Cosmopolitical Democracy', in *Debating Cosmopolitics*, p. 7.

11 Daniele Archibugi, 'Demos and Cosmopolis', in *Debating Cosmopolitics*, p. 262.

12 David Held, 'Democracy and the New International Order', in Daniele Archibugi and David Held (ed.), *Cosmopolitan Democracy: An Agenda for a New World Order*, Cambridge, Polity Press, 1995, p. 111.

13 David Held, 'The Transformation of Political Community: Rethinking Democracy in the Context of Globalization', in I. Shapiro and C. Hacker-Cordôn (eds), *Democracy's Edges*, Cambridge, Cambridge University Press, 1999, p. 105.

14 Ibid., p. 106.

15 Danilo Zolo, *Cosmopolis: Prospects for World Government*, Cambridge, Polity Press, 1997.

16 David Chandler, 'New Rights for Old? Cosmopolitan Citizenship and the Critique of State Sovereignty', *Political Studies*, Vol. 51, 2003, 332–49.

17 Ibid., p. 340.

18 Ibid., p. 343.

19 David Held, *Democracy and the Global Order*, Cambridge, Polity Press, 1995, p. 232.

20 David Held, *Global Covenant: The Social Democratic Alternative to the Washington Consensus*, Cambridge, Polity Press, 2004.

21 Ibid., p. 171.

22 My critique of 'governance' refers to the way this concept is used in the particular context of 'global governance'. There are of course other uses of this concept, as for instance in the case of different forms of 'network governance' where the aim is a widening of democratic contestation.

23 Urbinati, 'Can Cosmopolitical Democracy Be Democratic?', p. 80.

24 Robert Dahl, 'Can International Organizations Be Democratic? A Sceptic View', in *Democracy's Edges*, p. 25.

25 Ibid., p. 32.

26 Mary Kaldor, *Global Civil Society: An Answer to War*, Cambridge, Polity Press, 2003.

27 Ibid., p. 108.

28 Michael Hardt and Antonio Negri, *Empire*, Cambridge, MA, Harvard University Press, 2000.

29 Many books have already been published with very pertinent critiques of *Empire*. See for instance, Gopal Balakrishnan (ed.), *Debating Empire*, London Verso, 2004; Paul A. Passavant and Jodi Dean, (eds), *Empire's New Clothes*, New York Routledge, 2004, as well as the special issue of *Rethinking Marxism*, Vol. 13 3/4, 2001.

30 Michael Hardt and Antonio Negri, *Multitude, War and Democracy in the Age of Empire*, New York, Penguin Press, 2004.

31 Micheal Hardt and Antonio Negri, 'Adventures of the Multitude: Response of the Authors', in *Rethinking Marxism*, p. 239.

32 Hardt and Negri, 'Adventures of the Multitude', p. 242.

33 Michael Rustin, 'Empire: a Postmodern Theory of Revolution', in *Debating Empire*, p. 7.

34 Alberto Moreiras, 'A Line of Shadow: Metaphysics in Counter-Empire', in *Rethinking Marxism*, p. 224.

35 Hardt and Negri, *Empire*, p. 55.

36 Ibid., p. 361.

37 Doreen Massey, *For Space*, London Sage, 2005, chapter 14.

38 Michael Hardt and Antonio Negri, 'Globalization and Democracy', in Okwui Enwezor *et al.* (eds), *Democracy Unrealized*, Kassel, Hatje Cantz, 2002 p. 336.

39 Carl Schmitt, 'Die Einheit der Welt', Merkur, Vol. VI, 1 1952, pp. 1–11.

40 Massimo Cacciari, 'Digressioni su Impero e tre Rome', in: H. Frise, A. Negri and P. Wagner (eds), *Europa Politica Ragioni di una necessita*, Roma Manifestolibri, 2002.

41 A. Negri and D. Zolo, 'Empire and the Multitude: a Dialogue on the New Order of Globalization', *Radical Philosophy*, No. 120, July/August 2003, p. 33.

SIX CONCLUSION

1 Norberto Bobbio, *Destra e Sinistra: ragioni e significati di una distinzione politica*, Roma, Donzelli Editore, 1994.

2 Niklas Luhmann, 'The Future of Democracy', *Thesis Eleven*, No. 26, 1990, p. 51.

3 I have criticized the position of Rawls on this point in my book *The Return of the Political*, London, Verso, 1993, chapter 6.

4 For a discussion of those issues one can refer to William Kymlicka, *Multicultural Citizenship*, Oxford, Oxford University Press, 1995.

5 James Tully, 'Diverse Enlightenments', *Economy and Society*, Vol. 32, 3, August 2003, 501.

6 Ibid., p. 502.

7 Boaventura de Sousa Santos, *Toward a New Common Sense: Law, Science and Politics in a Paradigmatic Transition*, London, Routledge, 1995, p. 337–42.

8 Raimundo Panikkar, 'Is the Notion of Human Rights a Western Concept?', *Diogenes*, No. 120, 1982, pp. 81–2.

9 For a good overview of those positions see H. Frise, A. Negri and P. Wagner (eds), *Europa Politica Ragioni di una necessità*, Roma Manifestolibri, 2002. See in particular the introduction, pp. 7–18.

10 See for instance Jürgen Habermas, *The Postnational Constellation*, Cambridge, Polity Press, 2001, chapter 4.